A Barefoot Life:
A Memoir

Ardoth Hardin Wilkerson

Text Design: Lauren Wilkerson
Cover Design: Lauren Wilkerson
2011 Photos.com, a division of Getty Images
Creative Photo & Digital Imaging, Fort Myers, FL

Printed in the United States of America
by CREATESPACE a division of Amazon
First Edition/First Printing
Library of Congress Cataloging-in-Publication Data
LCCN: 2011905596
ISBN: 13: 978-1461045977
ISBN-10: 1461045975

This book is dedicated to those who take me into their lives through the sharing of my words. A special dedication goes to my daughter-in-law, Pam, who gave me a journal in 2000.

I have carried the journal for all these years and have read these words often.

Ardoth, may this journal inspire you to write that best seller. Many happy thoughts. We love you.

DON'T QUIT
Don't quit when the tide is lowest,
For it's just about to turn;
Don't quit over doubts and questions,
For there is something you may learn.
Don't quit when the night is darkest,
For it's just a while 'til dawn;
Don't quit when you've run the farthest,
For the race is almost run.
Don't quit when the hill is steepest,
For your goal is almost nigh;
Don't quit for you are not a failure
Until you fail to try.

--Jill Wolf

Love and hugs to "Pooh." Lauren, my precious granddaughter, has proofread, helped revise, shared thoughts, typed and typed and typed. I remain pleased and honored to have utilized her knowledge and advice to complete this book.

I am a creature of a day, passing through life as an arrow through the air. I am a spirit come from God and returning to God: Just hovering over the great gulf; 'til, a few moments hence, I am no more seen; I drop into an unchangeable eternity!

--John Wesley

Our Attitude is the Master of our Outcome

--Ardoth Hardin Wilkerson

INTRODUCTION

For, usually and fitly, the presence of an introduction is held to imply that there is something of consequence and importance to be introduced.

--Arthur Machen

I realize that I am mortal. When I depart from this Earth, I don't want to leave just an empty chair at the Christmas dinner table. The memories and thoughts that bounce around in my head daily define who I am. This book is my way of sharing these memories and thoughts with anyone who may want to laugh with me, cry with me, sympathize with me or even condemn me. Most importantly, my hope is that folks may not just enjoy the journey but identify in some positive way with my life's challenges and triumphs.

Some names have been changed, not to protect the innocent, but to protect me in case I were to tell a truth that someone doesn't want published.

I am amazed at the memories of my childhood which have slipped through my brain like sand through a sieve. I guess the memories which remain are the larger more important events that would not sift through the tiny holes. I am amazed at the emotions I allowed to fade away, but I am happy that I can still feel many of them as I recall my youth. All my memories may not be as exact as the experience, but they are simply what I revisit in my mind.

I was named after Mom's dear friend from Detroit. Mom had vowed to never have a passel of kids, but she promised her friend that if she ever had a girl, she would name her Ardoth. I became the seventh of eight children born to Grace Dean Cook Hardin and Ernest Woodward Hardin. I am the second daughter, and it still remains a mystery as to why I became the chosen one. My name served its purpose well in our family setting. I never missed a call to supper, a firm scolding or my time to dry dishes. However, as I ventured from the family circle to the academic and social scenes, I realized that my given name is unusual.

My first day of school, I returned home and informed Mom that I would not be able to learn anything from my teacher because she could not even spell my name. Mrs. Render, the poor speller, turned out to be a kind, influential, intelligent teacher, among the many who served as positive role models for most of my school days.

I shared this introduction with a few of my family members. Each critiqued with honesty. They did not tiptoe through my written words; instead, they waded in flat footed and stepped on some of what I thought were my sacred life scenes. One said, "Mom, we are really excited that we are going to hear secrets from your life, but you must present 'grabbers,' so a general audience will want to continue past the introduction."

I thought I had accomplished that writing feat until I re-read my words for the thousandth time. The "real meat" for the introduction remained in my head, still bouncing around waiting for the big scenes to be incorporated into the body of my book. I also realized that I was afraid I may even turn off potential readers who are tiring of the tell-all childhood books.

I have lived through, lived with, lived near, dealt with and experienced wonderful love, attempted molestations, family homicides, teen pregnancy, mentally challenged family members, family isolation, alcoholism, homelessness, school dropouts, serious auto accidents, and depression.

December 1960, I sat on my bed at my home in Western Kentucky. I stared at my flat smooth fifteen-year-old stomach. My boyfriend and I had just returned from the doctor's office where we discovered that we were having a baby. At that point in my life, I only had a suspicion as to how that little thing got there. I figured it had to be the very close interaction that we had when we parked on the back roads. My concern turned to terror as I wondered how in the world this child was going to join us without doing some major damage to me.

In 1960, we had no pamphlets, brochures, TV or radio to educate the youth about sex. My parents never used the word. So when we went on a date, I did what I thought everyone else was doing.

As you begin this journey with me, please notice that my aspirations and inspirations come from being able to take the "me" out of equations and embrace hope. Almost every decision I make in my life is made because I know that "this too shall pass." When the scenario is positive, I try to make it last and make it memorable. If the scenario is negative, I pray for a guiding hand, grasp it, and hang on for dear life.

CHAPTER 1

MY EARLIEST MEMORY

I think, at a child's birth, if a mother could ask a fairy godmother to endow it with the most useful gift, that gift should be curiosity

--Eleanor Roosevelt

My pastor suggested that I might have come out of the womb savoring a pork chop or a piece of southern fried chicken. Maybe! I do know that since my delivery as a Gemini on June 3rd, 1945, I have savored life with all of my God-given five senses and have even developed a few of my own.

Folks say that I cannot possibly remember April 13th, 1948, since I was only three years old. But I can even remember, what I now call, some of the many aromas of life. The acrid, eye-smarting odor of antiseptic alcohol, the baby powder, and the faint scent of the mantle lamp fumes are still real to me. The living room/bedroom of our small five-room home served as a waiting area for most of the Hardin clan that eventful night. The larger bedroom had become a delivery room.

My scrawny frame perched on one of my brother's knees. We were silent; a lone coal oil lamp burned at half-wick on the old wooden mantle top. However, the adjoining bedroom cast brighter light, interrupted occasionally by wavy, dancing, human shadows.

Where was Mom?

I just wanted Mom!

Suddenly, a piercing scream jarred every part of my being. Deep moans echoed through both rooms. I then knew where Mom was! The answer to one mystery just presented another. Why was Mom uttering such strange, scary sounds? A new, still strange, pleasant din of smiling voices, and a tiny meowing, sputtering noise interrupted the silence.

I do not remember contemplating my escape; I just remember bolting toward those mysterious shadows and sounds. I skidded through the doorway, but before I could reach the bed, my eyes set upon what I thought was a shiny baby doll resting on a marble-top dresser. The doll moved! Suddenly, a strong arm scooped me up and deposited me back on a knee in the now darker waiting room.

Finally, the shadowy figures became human forms as they, one by one, emerged from the bedroom. Sharing whispers, smiles, back pats, and handshakes, most folks said their goodbyes.

My brother carried me to the now pale-lighted mystery room. Placing a hush-finger across his lips, he placed me softly on the bed behind Mom, whose eyes fluttered between wake and sleep. My curiosity became anger. I imagine thinking, *Who is this red-*

faced, wrinkled skin, mouse squeaking midget, snuggled in my place on my Mom's arm? I had wallowed the waddle on her fleshy arm until it was a perfect fit for my head only. The little invader seemed to be trying to hide from me under one of her ample breasts. Exhaustion extinguished my emotions   and senses as I quickly fell asleep hanging over Mom's warm, powder perfumed back.

Later, Mom and others answered some of the questions about Janice Jane (Jaybug) Hardin's arrival as the last of eight children, five boys and three girls. Janice was not hiding from me; she was nursing. When I gave birth to two sons, I knew the reason for the moans.

GRANDMA COOK AND ARDOTH

CHAPTER 2

MY FAMILY

They...threw themselves into the interests of the rest, but each showed his or her own furrow. Their thoughts, their little passions and hopes and desires, all ran along separate lines. Family life is like this- animated, but collateral.

--Rose Macauly

Everyone should keep a journal and/or write a book. I regret that I did not ask more questions about my parents' young lives. I learned that they met while Dad painted a house just down the street from Mom's home. I wonder how Mom and Dad dressed for their wedding.

Having no photos or passed-down stories, I must just imagine them holding hands while walking the trails and paths in McLean County, Kentucky. All of my grandparents passed away before I arrived except for Grandma Cook, my Mother's Mom. She died when I was eleven months old, so I have no memory of her. Thus, I was not privileged to know a grandparent's importance in my life. My parents have passed and so have all of my Aunts and Uncles.

Being an avid reader and writer, I have my own prerequisites that contribute to my enjoyment of a writing and reading. I do not like to find characters introduced sporadically throughout a book unless it is essential to the plot. The following are the precious folks who will be with us on our journey.

Grace Dean Cook Hardin, Mom, came from a medium sized family of three boys and two girls. She and her brothers and sister were the products of a second marriage. Grandpa, Mom's father William Cook, who was a Methodist minister, produced eleven children by his first marriage. He married my grandmother when he was fifty-five and Grandma was only twenty-three. He then died at the age of sixty-six, leaving Grandma with five children to raise.

Mom suffered from the tough times after grandpa's death. She vowed to never have lots of children, but the good Lord saw things differently and blessed them with eight youngsters.

Ernest Woodward Hardin Sr., Dad, came from a large family of eleven. He married Mom in Daviess County, Kentucky on April 23rd, 1928. Dad was twenty-two and Mom was eighteen. Because of many factors that sometimes divide people, they separated in 1956. They never divorced and maintained a civil, close family relationship until God called Dad home on November 2^{nd,} 1965, and Mom on September 2nd, 1993.

Gary Houston, on April 21st, 1929, became the first

born child of Ernest and Grace Hardin. Three boys followed, Oliver Lee, July 26th, 1931; Delman Ray, September 22nd, 1933; Ernest Woodward Jr., May 4th, 1936. Yvonne (Vonnie) became their first girl, born December 28th, 1940. Another boy, Dudley Eugene, sneaked in September 11th, 1942. Last but, of course, important, were two more girls, Ardoth Margaret (yours truly) June 3rd, 1945, and on May 13th, 1948, the baby of our family, Janice Jane (Jaybug), came along.

Ardoth Hardin Wilkerson

CHAPTER 3

HOME COOKING

Youth fades; love droops; the leaves of friendship fall;
A Mother's secret hope outlives them all.

--Oliver Wendell Homes

We all shared chores as soon as we were deemed capable. For me that time came at around five years of age. I wanted to be Mom's shadow, and I am thankful that she put her shadow to learning early. We arose around 5 a.m. The first order of business was a trip to the outhouse. Our home had no electricity and no running water inside. We were fortunate to have a hydrant in the corner of our front yard. We were also fortunate to have a two-holer out back. Many families with the one-holer meant that someone stood outside in the dark or cold waiting for her turn. Early toilet time meant that the other folks had not been there to "stir up the air." The early users also had a better choice of wiping material. Catalog order pages were not slick and were kinder to one's hind part. I once hid some of these special pages under the lime bucket, but somehow lime got on my special paper. I almost burned myself a new hind hole. That smarted for a week.

Mom and I slipped quietly back into the house to wash our hands and began preparing breakfast for the large crew. She always placed the kindling in the stove just right so the fire could breathe and ignite the larger pieces of wood. At five years of age, it was an adventure to stand on my stool, make a big doodlebug hole in the flour, squeeze in some lard, then watch Mom add just enough buttermilk to form a large soft ball of dough. I was older before I could roll out the dough, and Mom had her special way to get the most biscuits from the first cutting to avoid reshaping the dough often. She removed the bread pan from the oven where she had placed it to melt a big dollop of lard. I watched her artfully roll out the mixture on the well-floured biscuit board, then firmly push the metal biscuit cutter into the fluffy soft mound, causing little puffs of white flour to escape from the two holes in the side of the cutter. With a deft twist of her wrist, a perfectly formed biscuit emerged, which she skillfully removed with her left hand and greased both sides of the delicacy to place it in the warm baking tin. The dip in the grease helped to produce biscuits that had a subtle brown top, fluffy middle, and crispy bottom. Her right hand continued the cutting routine, with only a small change in the sequence as she dug the cutter into the flour occasionally to keep the dough from sticking.

If we were serving bacon, Mom cut off the rind and

made slits in the sides so that the meat would not curl as it fried. I was not allowed to work with the hot stove until I was about ten. I carefully carried the silverware, dishes, and butter to the table. Mom prepared the meat, gravy, and eggs. Tea steeped on the back of the stove in a pan holding a metal pod filled with black tea flakes. I do not remember coffee, but I am sure the adults drank it.

I suppose the breakfast aromas awakened the rest of the family. They would stumble through the kitchen, head for the outhouse, come back through to wash hands, then seat themselves at the table laden with fluffy, brown biscuits, fried meat, fried eggs, gravy, real butter, homemade blackberry jam, and if in season, fresh sliced tomatoes.

While clearing the breakfast table, we started lunch or what we called dinner. We referred to our meals as breakfast, dinner, and supper. Usually by 9 a.m., a pot of green beans, pinto beans, navy beans, or northern beans, which were seasoned with meat grease from the fried breakfast bacon or sausage drippings, simmered atop the old stove. Most of our meat dishes consisted of fried rabbit, squirrel, fish or chicken. We also enjoyed rabbit dumplings, squirrel dumplings or chicken dumplings. Occasionally, we could afford bologna, ham or chops. I was ten years old before I tasted ground beef. I thought I had died and gone to heaven. If we grew hungry before the next meal, we uncovered the goodies from the previous meal, which were left on the dining table. By the age of ten, with supervision, I could cook a meal, clean the house, and help with laundry.

I learned how to take the starched clothes from the

drying line while they were still damp and roll them up so that I could iron them easily. If I didn't catch them before they were too dry, I had to dip my hands into a pan of water to sprinkle them. We finally modernized the wetting method by using a bottle sprinkler. I learned how to use the iron which I had removed from a piece of hot tin that had been placed over an open fire. I used the hottest irons for the starched clothes. As the irons cooled, I pressed the easier to iron, un-starched laundry.

I don't recall fussing about my learning times. I felt special when I helped.

When I tell folks that I remember only one whipping in my life, they are skeptical. I don't recall the circumstances surrounding the event, but I will never forget the grand finale. I circled the outside of the house a few time with Mom in close pursuit. I finally detoured into a field of tall weeds that separated us from a garage on 431. I squatted low and stayed just far enough into the jungle so that I still had a view of the house.

She just stood there, a long keen switch hanging from one hand. Then to my utter relief, she left. Just as I had mustered up the nerve to move, she reappeared carrying a chair. There she sat, waiting. Mom knew I would never go to the garage or to the highway without permission. None of the other kids were in sight, nor would they be as long as there was a switch involved. Not only did I have no desire for a taste of that skinny limb, I also did not plan to return to that house until Mom had cooled down a bit.

I'm not sure how much time passed. I just knew that I was winning until...it first crawled across my foot. I didn't see it. Then a green fluorescent fly set up camp on a stem of darker green grass. It pranced and flitted around, never taking its eyes off me. Some choice! I could remain in the field with the creepy bugs or emerge to the sure encounter with a mad old woman. I'm still not sure how she caught me. I'm sure my feet were barely touching the ground as I literally flew out of my sanctuary after being joined by a two pound honey bee.

It hurt! I remember!

Ardoth Hardin Wilkerson

CHAPTER 4

LEARNING DAZE

It is important that students bring a ragamuffin, barefoot irreverence to their studies; they are not here to worship what is known, but to question it.

--Jacob Bronowski

My academic journey began September 1951, as a first grader at Livermore High School. Livermore School educated students from grades one through twelve. There was no kindergarten in 1951 in McLean County.

Mrs. Render, our first grade teacher set a wonderful example of a compassionate, caring person. That example held true for all of my educational leaders at LHS. After our name-spelling problem, the first day of school, I learned she was a wise lady. I hope she realized the important role she played in teaching me to be a better student and person.

One lesson I learned from her was to do what the

teacher asks me to do. Just before recess one day, a classmate could not find her spelling book. Mrs. Render told us to open our desks to see if we had the student's property. I knew I did not take the book, so I sat smugly watching my fellow students open desks and search through their clutter for the speller. Mrs. Render walked to the front of my desk and sternly asked why I had not done as I had been told to do. I replied, "I didn't take Jeannine's speller."

She said, "I am not accusing anyone of taking the book. It could have been placed in the wrong desk."

Slowly, while all eyes peered my way, I eased the top from the desk. There, staring back at me, were two spelling books. Mrs. Render opened both books.

Student name: Ardoth Hardin.

Student name: Jeannine Frashure.

My fellow students climbed the monkey bars, played red rover, and pushed the merry-go-round without me during recess. I also did not tell Mom or Dad when I arrived home about my incident. In those days, teachers were not automatically blamed for a student's problems. This student took responsibility for her behavior or faced punishment at school and at home.

By the time I entered second grade, I realized that no one else in the school or probably in the whole state, maybe the world, had the name my Mom had bestowed upon me. It pleased me, however, that Miss Morton spelled my complete name without hesitation.

Miss Morton lived in a two story house in the middle of town. I always felt that the huge white structure held many secrets that we kids would never discover. I never ventured into her yard, walked near her windows or even sat on her steps which bordered the city sidewalk. I don't recall her being mean to anyone; she just seemed to teach us and then disappear until the next school day when she rang the loud bell which sat on the corner of her large wooden desk.

One day Miss Morton rang her tardy bell and all were quiet except for me. I continued to tell a friend something important, I'm sure. My teacher scolded me, but later in the quiet study period, I talked. This time I had pushed her too far. She removed her sign from the desk drawer and hung it around my neck, then deposited me in the hall outside the door entrance. The sign read something like, "I cannot remain silent in class." As soon as Miss Morton stepped back into the classroom, I turned the sign over. Guess what was written on the other side!

After a trip upstairs, we were returning to our second-grade room when a friend and I glanced down from the stairwell. Miss Morton stood below us. I had never seen the top of her head. To my amazement, tracing along the top, at the part in her very black hair, there was a very white streak. My first thought was something about a skunk. I showed my new mystery to my friend. She informed me that Miss Morton dyed her hair. As you will discover throughout this book, I learn many of the worldly things the hard way. I asked, "What does that mean?"

Jean said, "She puts black shoe polish on her white hair."

This would need some more explanation for me to believe such a silly tale. As soon as she rang her quiet-time bell, I raised my hand. She called on me. I asked just because I needed to know, "Jean says you dye your white hair with black shoe polish."

Silence reigned supreme!

All eyes turned toward me. I didn't notice Jean's reaction, but now as an adult looking back, I'm sure she must have fainted and fallen to the floor forming a quivering heap of terrified flesh.

Miss Morton's next words came haltingly from her blazing red face, "Students, take out your books and read." She motioned for me to follow her to the hallway. Still not knowing that I had said anything wrong, my thoughts may have been that she planned to explain to me her reason for dying white hair. Instead, she just stared at me for a while, and then asked, "Ardoth, do you realize that the question you asked me was very rude?"

"No," I answered. Miss Morton calmly explained the importance of being sure that the questions one asks should not be harmful or hurtful. I explained to her that I did not mean to be rude or hurtful; I had just never heard of someone putting black stuff on her hair. My seven-year-old mind had not been muddled by words like, "vanity or modesty," so I didn't really understand the complete lesson she tried to convey. I did learn to never ask another teacher whether she dyed her hair.

A small circus came to town one summer. These odd strangers set up their show on the street in front of Miss Morton's house. I mainly recall a few clowns, cotton candy, and various animals.

A baby elephant, attached to a rope with a man at the other end, walked in a circle that had been cordoned off with more rope. Kids could ride for a small sum. I had no desire to get on that stinky thing, but evidently someone paid for me because the rope man came to me, gripped me under the arms and deposited my bony butt on the elephant's back. Even though a dirty, old rug draped his back, his sharp spiny hairs poked my tender skin. Unhappy did not describe how I felt. Scared to high heaven would have come close. The creature had not made a sound all evening, but he chose to make his presence known as we made our second or third circle by Miss Morton's house. It threw up its long spout, opened its toothless mouth and bellowed. I guess he also wanted to show off a little for the crowd, so he did a side step toward the bystanders. Everyone screamed and cleared the area except the rope holder, Miss Morton, and yours truly. While the gray, bristle brush I was riding continued to entertain the crowd, Miss Morton walked to the corner of her porch to check on the commotion. She looked directly into my face, and instead of entertaining thoughts of my possible rescue, she smiled and waved. By the last round, the elephant had settled into his calm easy gait around the circle. I guess the folks thought I had been part of a planned performance. They applauded loudly and shouted words like, "Way to go; that was great." With my new celebrity status, I bragged about how easily I had accomplished the feat. They didn't notice that when the gentleman removed me from the elephant's back, I was actually so frightened and stiff that he had to try twice to get me to straighten my bowed legs and loosen by grip on a wrinkle in the elephant's back.

I remembered Miss Morton's lesson concerning rudeness, but it didn't keep me from telling my class that a substitute teacher had false teeth. I don't recall the grade I was in, but this time I knew I was being rude because I was angry and sticking my nose in where it did not belong, again. Most students tried to give the substitutes a rough time. I usually felt sorry for the young lady substitutes. Actually, it was a treat to listen to someone new because our teachers were seldom absent.

Larry began a conversation whispering, "I bet that lady has false teeth." The boys chuckled. I ignored the mounting fun.

Suddenly, the lady rapped a paddle on the desk. "Someone has stolen the lunch money which was here on the corner of this desk!" No one spoke. All eyes forward. "Who was the last person standing by this corner?"

Silence!

Then, someone said, "I saw Marcie by your desk."

Marcie was always so alone, quiet. Because of her sadness and lack of friends, I felt sorry for her. I never tried to help her because I guess I just didn't know how to begin. The substitute called Marcie to the front of the room. She walked in her usual slump, no expression on her face, and in no hurry. Then, the teacher started yelling at her and for the first time, I saw her cry.   Everyone remained still as robots, except, guess who? I cried too. Again, all eyes stared toward me, as, without even knowing where the words came from, I burst out, "Marcie wouldn't steal your old money, and besides that, you have false teeth."

Instead of mass laughter, there was a waiting game. The sub tried to analyze the whole situation. Marcie moon-eyed me, and I just sat there wondering whose voice that sounded just like mine had come from my direction. Time did not fly by. Time stood still and so did everyone in that classroom. Now that the sub's focus had changed, Marcie made the first move and walked back to her desk. The sub looked at me and pointed to the door.

She said, "Do not return to this classroom!"

I spent the rest of the period in the girls' restroom. I had plenty of time to worry and wonder, but all that really resulted from the incident was that I made a new friend and some of the students thought I was cool. Some thought that I just didn't have all my marbles. Thankfully, that incident never reached home either.

Ardoth Hardin Wilkerson

CHAPTER 5

P RIDGE

Having been poor is no shame, but being ashamed of it, is.

--Benjamin Franklin

My introduction to sex actually began as soon as I was old enough to play in the thicket and the pigpen. The abandoned pigpen provided a barren, dusty, deep rutted playground for a bunch of barefoot kids. We loved the soft dust, half-dead bushes and large tree roots which had been exposed by the rutting of the former residents. There was nothing like splashing barefoot through silky soft dirt, until we disturbed a resting bumble bee.

The thicket offered a small shady grove of tall, twisted, bug bearing trees for us to climb, swing on grapevines and generally do our best to break a bone or two. The older siblings took on the task of supervising the younger as we tarzaned throughout the small forest or created a mini dust bowl as we rampaged through the pigpen behind our home on P Ridge. I think we all bounced very well, because I remember no breaks, but we had plenty of stings which were immediately attended to with wet baking soda, a dab of wet tobacco or coal oil.

These areas remained off limits unless we were told that we could go there and play for about an hour. How did we earn these awesome trips to our favorite playground? I didn't figure out that mystery until I learned about sex and came to the gruesome conclusion that Mom and Dad actually engaged in such activities. We always stayed until we could hear Mom yell for us or sometimes Dad would come to send us home as he headed to the creek to raise his fish nets.

One day, I fell from a large tree branch which I thought would provide a comfortable bed for my dinky body. I hit the hard ground flat and it knocked the breath out of me. After I recovered to the point that I could run, I headed home in a hurry. I hit the back door in a run and bounced off. Still crying, I rushed to the front door only to find it locked. I knocked furiously for what seemed like forever. An unhappy, stringy haired Dad finally came to the door. After inspecting my back, and I guess thinking I would live, he sent me back to play. I did not have even the slightest notion as to what my parents were doing at that time. Our playtime, it seems, was also our parents' playtime.

When I hear of youngsters being bored today, I recall how we knew that around every corner we could find or make a new adventure, even if it was in a pigpen. Bored was not a word in our vocabulary.

Evidently, I grew up poor. I did not really think about it as a child. Folks across town had bigger houses, but I honestly recall only a few times in my young life when I wondered about material wealth.

One occasion was when my girlfriend, Carolyn, and her Mammy came to visit. Their grandmother, Mrs. Bertha Green, also known as Mammy, was raising Carolyn and her brother, Larry. This day Carolyn was eating from a box of Cracker Jacks. Any snack foods were a treat for us since we seldom had them. I wanted some Cracker Jacks; I wanted to know what exciting prize lounged around inside that shiny, sweet smelling box of candied popcorn. Mammy disciplined Carolyn. She threw her box of Cracker Jacks on the floor where they scattered like tiny, soft, sugar rocks across the linoleum. My muscles moved before my mind as I leaned forward in my chair. One glimpse of Mom's face relayed an unmistakable message. "Don't even think about it!"

I did see the prize; I just do not recall what it was. After a swift swat on the butt, Carolyn reluctantly began picking up the kernels and pitching them into the box. To my great horror, she threw the box, prize included, into the coal bucket. I did not need another message from Mom.

An eternity later, they left. That box, which sat upright on top of the chunks of coal, never left my mind during the rest of our visit. This was also one of the times that I realized Moms are mind readers. She sauntered to the coal bucket, leaned down, retrieved the box of Cracker Jacks, prize included, raised the top on the stove and dropped it in. I recall almost her exact words. "We may be poor, but we don't have to eat other people's trash." I am sure she never considered the prize which meant as much to me as the candy popcorn.

Another incident that caused me to wonder about our financial station in life was when the car coats were popular. I have never been a fashion queen, but those coats were the neatest things since I had discovered jeans. I begged, I begged, and I begged. Finally, when my coat could not be mended again, Mom ordered me a car coat. I hurried to the post office every afternoon to check for my delivery. When it arrived, it was the most beautiful brick red with white stitching and, of course, sported those whisky-barrel buttons.

I did not walk to school the next day; I floated on red coat wings. I just knew everyone would be happy for me and that everyone would love my coat. My joy was evident to all of my classmates. Some wanted to try it on, some just smiled, but one girl came to me to feel of the sleeves. She said, "This is not a real car coat. Feel of mine. It is thick and soft. You can't afford a real one anyway."

We went to our classes, but all I could think about was that new coat hanging in the closet in the back of the room. I did not want someone to make fun of me at recess, but I wanted so much to wear it out to play. I reluctantly slipped it on.

On the playground, the kids seesawed, jumped rope, played red rover, etc. I scanned the crowd to see who paid attention to me. Finally, my best friend, Jean, found me, and I asked Jean again if she liked my coat. She told me she did so that helped to get me through the day. I didn't wonder why we could not afford a better coat for me. I just snuggled into mine each cold day and it kept me warm.

The value of money to me, until I became older, meant that I could buy some stick pretzels, Hesmer's potato chips or maybe a creamy, malted Cho-Cho.

Ardoth Hardin Wilkerson

CHAPTER 6

DAD

There's something like a line of gold thread running through a man's words when he talks to his daughter, and gradually over the years it gets to be long enough for her to pick it up in her hands and weave into a cloth that feels like love itself.

--John Gregory Brown

The first hobo I ever saw came to our door just as we had finished supper. Dad directed him to the back door where Mom fixed him a plate of food. I could not take my eyes off the ragged man. This hobo turned out to be a revenue man looking for local bootleggers or moon shiners. I don't know the results of that visit, but according to Dad as we talked years later, that was one way the law investigated illegal alcohol sales. One of our neighbors sold bootleg liquor. There may have been other drugs available in the area during the 1940's through 1970's, but I know that I was at least twenty years old before I even heard the word "marijuana."

My Dad, as many men in our little county, enjoyed moonshine and whiskey. And, as most, he enjoyed liquor in excess. Some were open with their imbibing, while others confined their indulgences to their homes. Alcohol was the drug of choice in our area because it was cheap, plentiful, and fairly accepted as norm if one didn't cause too many "obvious" problems. I must define "obvious." If folks got drunk and caused trouble in public, the law would try to settle the problem by taking the parties home. You may guess who took care of the problem from there. If the men did not cooperate, they were put in jail to sober up.

I never entered the Livermore jail, but I remember taking Dad unfiltered Camel cigarettes and food until he would come home in a few hours. What is so odd to me is that I can recall many emotions of my childhood, but many I cannot. If there were shame or sadness in me as I gave Dad his necessities, I simply do not remember. I also don't remember all reasons for my Dad being in jail, but I know that he was a kind, witty, intelligent man unless he was drinking, then he became an angry person. Dad stood only about 5' 6" tall, but he became as dangerous as a buzz saw when he drank too much.

Dad took us for weekends at our cabin on Rough River. Since we never owned a car, only a truck, the whole family piled into the pick-up, which was also loaded with quilts, pillows, guns, fishing gear and food. I can remember fleeting pictures of those fun days. An oil pump worked at sucking the crude from the ground a short distance from the cabin. I would sneak a quilt or grass sack and head to the pump rod, throw the cover over the rod and ride until I was called to task by Mom or Dad. Mom would have us find a bushy bush so we could sweep the dirt floor which always felt cool to my bare feet. We carried straw or hay to spread over this large wooden bed that we slept on. It consisted of wooden legs holding up rough boards. We little ones climbed on the boards and spread the straw and the quilts. That was our family bed. At night, I fell asleep listening to the little varmints scurrying amongst the straw and the larger ones inspecting the new smells escaping through the cracks after Mom had cooked bacon or fried potatoes and onions. Dad and the boys caught fish and killed squirrels or rabbits. We ate well.

That peaceful retreat became the scene of family homicides.

Ardoth Hardin Wilkerson

CHAPTER 7

WHAT IF!

A plea from the mentally challenged: Don't call me crazy because I stare at you with vacant eyes. Help me and let me know you care. If medical attention doesn't resolve my handicap, don't dump me back into an unknowing society where they and I will be left to suffer the consequences of my illness.

--Ardoth Hardin Wilkerson

I have tried to use humor all my life to insulate me from the bad and the ugly. It works most of the time. I would rather have it this way then to cry through life with just occasional comic relief. There will never be comic relief for those who recall July 13th, 1950. By the end of that day, there were only seven members of the once ten-member Hardin family living at the foot of the 431 bridge.

This is the most difficult chapter for me to complete. I have asked myself often why I feel the need to share such an intimate family tragedy. My book began as a telling of my life for my children, grandchildren, and their grandchildren. To omit this chapter in my life would mean that I have not been completely true to my conviction to share my life as it was and is. My decision to write this chapter came a few years ago as I finally became sad and angry while listening to folks who use terms like, "He is a nut case or he should be in a loony bin." This attitude toward those who have mental challenges is prevalent throughout society. I cannot change all these attitudes, but I can express my feelings toward the gross injustices done to mentally ill people.

A few years ago, I suffered from a bout of severe depression. Only those who have truly been depressed can understand my mental state. True depression is not just being sad, unhappy or worried. It is the inability to mentally function. I understand why my doctor treated me for weeks before sending me to a specialist who confirmed my severe illness. After beginning a regimen of Cymbalta, I replaced the empty shell of a human being by becoming Ardoth again. Those three months in my life were such a blessing. Yes, I said, "They were a blessing."

I am now able to say, "Now I know." I know the helpless feelings of not being able to control my thoughts. I know how it feels to be completely isolated both physically and mentally from loved ones.

During those three months, I knew my mind was unstable, but I did not reach out to family and friends as usual. Knowing what mental illness can do to a family, I hesitated to share my malady. After consulting a physiatrist and beginning my road to wellness, I made another decision: to take on a crusade.

I noticed the facial expressions when I finally talked to folks about my new and wonderful doctor, a physiatrist. Some people did not even want to hear about my mind problem. My crusade began with the simple plan to express my dislike of the words used to refer to those who are mentally challenged. I have had to explain my attitude to folks many times. I have also relished their apologies. Old habits are hard to break. I know that is a song, but so true. As I share the story of our family crisis, I am continuing my quest to alter the hateful, hurtful reactions to mental illness.

Society in general is not the only culprit in this scenario. I had no energy, wanted to sleep often, and was not pleasant many times. My doctor diagnosed my illness as thyroid deficiency. He prescribed medication which corrected my illness. My insurance covered the costs as it does with most of my other medical problems, but it paid less for treatment of my mental illness.

While speaking with a friend about mental illness, she reminded me that a person treated for thyroid problems was not dangerous to society. True! This just presents an argument in favor of more funds to study this illness, more understanding that mentally ill people do not ask for this terrible sickness, and to provide adequate, caring, treatment to protect the patient and society.

My eldest brother, Gary, became despondent as a teen. He spent some time in Western State Mental Hospital, in Hopkinsville, Kentucky. Upon returning home, he expressed his desire to stay in the cabin we used on Rough River. There he hunted, fished, and family members took him supplies.

The morning of July 13th, 1950, Delman and Junior gathered their containers to head to the blackberry patches, most of which were along the river banks and many near the old cabin. Mom asked the boys to take Eugene, who was seven years old, so that they may get enough berries for a good canning. Eugene had other important plans such as throwing dirt clods, playing with the dogs, or pestering his sisters. Junior asked Mom to allow his little brother to just stay home and play.

Delman and Junior walked to Rough River where they paddled across to take supplies to their brother.

There is no chronological order to what my five-year-old mind comprehended that terrible day. Standing on tiptoes, I set dishes on the lunch table while Mom cooked. I remember words from Mom like, "I wonder where the boys are? They should have been home by now." My next flash was of Gary leaning against the mantle, his gun propped beside him. He sobbed.

Later, I sat on the corner of a bed and watched Mom and Dad holding each other. I had never seen them hug before. My image of them today brings to mind Norman Rockwell paintings which always concentrate on movement and facial expressions. Their faces twisted in agony as they seemed to cling to each other as if they were trying to keep from falling to the floor.

I have no memory of sadness or fear during those days, just excitement because of the unusual. I touched a shiny piece of metal on the chest of a man who rocked me to sleep. Strange people invaded every corner of our home. Lights flashed on the 431 highway which is a main road north and south through McLean county.

I entered a sweet smelling room that had two tall beds with sides on them. I guess, thinking they were sleeping, I climbed one side of a casket to reach my brother. Someone removed me from the room.

Gary was declared criminally insane and placed in a secure mental facility. I am so glad that my mind is incapable of even imagining the loss of one of my children, so I surely never felt the anguish which Mom and Dad suffered that night. How surreal to have to lie down and close their eyes with the day's events haunting them. I lost three brothers in one night. They lost three sons in one night. Yes, Gary was lost to them, but how did they grieve for him when he had taken their other sons from them?

If our world had been as media mobile then, as now, we would have been top news nationwide. Thank goodness that did not happen.

Delman's class ring arrived a few months after his death. Yvonne, Janice and I, by the grace of youthful innocence, were sheltered from the daily anguish that the rest of my family surely suffered. Dad never forgave Gary. He tried to drown his broken world with alcohol. My parents continued to raise a two-year-old, a five-year-old, a Down syndrome ten-year-old and two sons who had also lived through the terrible loss.

Forgetting my three brothers was easy for me. Gary had spent time away from home at Hopkinsville Mental Hospital before the incident. And I am sure as teens, Delman and Junior, like most of the Hardins, roamed the woods and river banks when they were not in school, so I have fleeting mental glimpses of their existence. As an adult, I often ponder how in the world Mom and Dad coped with the challenge of his never being able to forgive Gary and of her communicating with Gary.

I cannot recall how I learned the details of my brothers' deaths. I believe it was a gradual accumulation of information which I finally pieced together from Mom's mailings, listening to her talk with her friends, news clippings, and two school annuals dedicated to my brothers. Absolutely no one in our close family spoke of the incident.

I do not know Mom's thoughts as the years went by, nor do I recall when I first noticed that she sent small packages in the mail. Letters arrived addressed to her in crooked almost indistinguishable hand writing. One letter from Gary rambled on about a surgeon poking around in his head. Mom later learned that a doctor had performed a lobotomy on her son. I watched her cry as she read the letters. I watched her carefully wrap socks, handkerchiefs, candy and other small items in the boxes. As soon as I was allowed to go to town alone, I mailed the boxes and was instructed to take the letters directly to her.

The last memory I had of Gary was his return to our home that fateful night until 1963. I took Mom to see her son. They had not seen each other for many years. My first glimpse of Gary filled me with fear, sadness, love, and pain. My fear came from the details I had learned about the homicides. The sadness and pain came from the vacant stare in his piercing brown eyes. The love was because he was my brother and he was sick. Gary inherited Dad's sharp, chiseled face, and his freckles. Even though he stood and walked with shoulders slumped, he was taller than any other family member.

Dad passed away in 1965; he had not laid eyes on his son for fifteen years. Mom wanted Gary to see his Dad one last time. I remained torn by Dad's wishes to never see his son again and Mom wanting a memory of seeing her son and husband together again. I have made so many wrong decisions in life that I could fill a lengthy book. That was one decision I cannot judge. I have asked God to forgive me if I hurt people by taking Gary into the already emotional family scene. The family and folks, who certainly held horrible visions of 1950, viewed his presence differently than Mom and I. In my mind I imagined a cathartic scene of Dad and Gary sharing a forgiving moment.

Gary walked into the funeral parlor in handcuffs, peered down at Dad and sobbed. He was then led out immediately to a waiting vehicle which returned him to the mental hospital.

When the politicians decided to release thousands of mentally ill people into the streets, Gary was left to fend for himself. Mom and Yvonne lived alone. Mom loved Gary but still feared him. I could not ask Tommy to take him into our home. We both worked and were trying to raise two young sons. I also feared Gary's mind.

He roamed from one boarding house to another until he was finally jailed for assault of an elderly man whom Gary said had tried to take his money. We learned of this through a newspaper article that addressed the plight of the "forgotten people."

I helped Mom arrange for him to be admitted to a nursing home near McLean County where we visited him often. Gary died of a heat stroke in September, 1988.

"If" is one of the most powerful two letter words in the English language. It causes many reflective thoughts that can be painful unless we recognize that we cannot change the past. We can only learn from it.

What if Eugene had gone berry picking that day? What if the medical community had known more? What if Gary had not had a gun? I could go on and on, but instead, I just want those in the medical field and society to address mental illness as what it is. It is a sad, scary malady that most of the time we can only identify by the actions of the sufferers. We need to devote time, energy, and research into this illness.

A Barefoot Life

IN MEMORIAM

In memory of Delman Hardin, we the Seniors of 1951, dedicate this the twentieth edition of the L. H. S. Hi-Times in honor of a beloved and loyal classmate.

Although his physical form cannot be seen, treasured memory remains in the hearts and minds of all his classmates and all those who knew the value of a faithful friendship.

Delman Ray Hardin
1933-1950

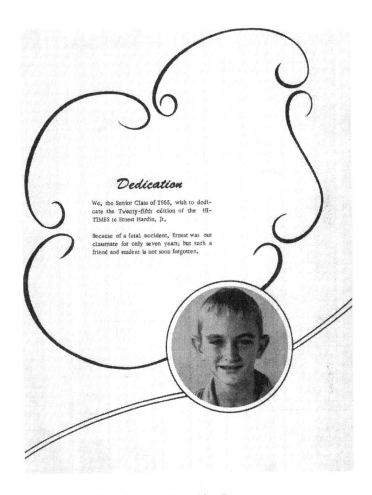

Dedication

We, the Senior Class of 1955, wish to dedicate the Twenty-fifth edition of the HI-TIMES to Ernest Hardin, Jr.

Because of a fatal accident, Ernest was our classmate for only seven years; but such a friend and student is not soon forgotten.

Ernest Woodward Hardin Jr.
1936-1950

Ardoth Hardin Wilkerson

CHAPTER 8

BE CAREFUL WHAT YOU ASK FOR!

Providence protects children and idiots. I know because I have tested it.

--Mark Twain

The clothes in my closet were purchased so that I may cover my body before appearing in public. The public is happy. I could have invented the phrase, "Clothes do not a person make." The evolution of my clothes closet has come full circle. I discovered jeans and shirts but not the girly ones emblazoned with flowers or hearts. I donned boys' tees until the little knobs of maturity became obvious. Then I switched to button front shirts. Sundays for church and picture day at school, Mom insisted that I wear little lady clothes.

My hair had no color name. It wasn't blonde like Eugene's or dark like Yvonne's. I think someone referred to it as mousy brown. Not only was my hair color nameless, it sported a very visible cowlick where my right hairline met my forehead. I guess that ole cow worked me over. I recall Dad saying, "She's got freckles on her, but she's pretty."

Even if I layered hair on top of the cowlick, it just formed a round hump above my eye that left my face crooked. I decided one day that the easiest way to fix that problem was to get rid of it. I nipped it down to the scalp and then tried to pull the other hair over the empty spot. Didn't happen! That hair returned with a vengeance. It seemed to grow back thicker and stiffer.

I convinced Mom that if I had curls, I could cover the rebel hair, and she wouldn't need to work with it so much. At the age of eight, off to the beauty shop I went. I made that new venture alone, as I did most of them, because Mom had to be with my little sister and Yvonne.

I opened the beauty shop door and was accosted by an awful stench. I sat quietly in awe and fear as the elderly lady twisted another elderly lady's hair onto small, shiny, white cylinders. She then put the lady in another chair that had little ropes hanging from a round hood. Next, the beautician attached the ropes to the cylinders on the patron's head. The hair lady left for a long time. Lordy! I thought I had smelled the worst, but I had not. The odor of burned hair and an odor that singed my nose hairs permeated the room.

When the beauty shop lady returned, she washed my hair over a big sink, toweled it, and began twisting my locks around the same type of rods that she had used earlier. I wanted to cover my nose and face, but I wanted to be grown-up too. I waited while she released the red- faced perspiring, hanging lady. I eased onto a chair, but the ropes wouldn't reach so she placed a booster under me and hooked each rod to a rope. The other lady left and my shop lady disappeared too. I waited, immovable and hot. The smell of smoldering hair had to be coming from my head. Then I heard slight sparking noises. But, I must have thought this woman knew what she was doing, so I waited. Finally, she reappeared and seemed to be in a hurry to release me.

I stared into the mirror. I had no reference to compare to my new hair-do. I only remember that she offered me a scarf to wear home. Looking back, I guess she wanted me to get as far away from her place of business before someone spotted me. I had imagined my hair as soft blonde curls, bouncing around my head as I jumped rope or ran the softball bases. I suppose I thought the perm would curl and color. Didn't happen!

I gladly wrapped the scarf over my new fuzz and scurried home. I don't remember whether Mom laughed or cried. She just stared--forever. I think she uttered some not so nice words and then she said we could fix it. The only positive outcome was that the cowlick now looked like the rest of my singed, kinked hair. I guess Mom repaired it. I know we rolled it on clothes pins and rubber bands that night, but I don't recall my clothes-pin hair do the next day.

One would think that I would never go near another perm or beauty shop, but I did and I have all my life. I have had perms in shops from Maine to California. I still have a cowlick, but I have learned the art of backcombing to tame the rebel hair.

Ardoth Hardin Wilkerson

CHAPTER 9

JUST COUNTRY

The things which the child loves remain in the domain of the heart until old age. The most beautiful thing in life is that our souls remain over the places where we once enjoyed ourselves.

--Kahlil Gibran

I leave pieces of my heart at many places I have lived or visited. A big chunk of my happiness remains in Ohio County, Kentucky. After one of my parents' separations, they reconciled and Dad tried to begin a better life without alcohol.

Now, how happy could one skinny, boney, freckled-faced tomboy be? Very! The beautiful, meandering, Green River provided the view from the backyard. The east yard bordered the long, winding, Rogrine slough. Since three years of age, I have relished every minute I spend on a creek, slough, river or any body of water that may give up a few fish.

I believe that I can share so many memories of that time because I filled my days embracing the real country family life: feed the chickens, milk the cow, fish, raise a garden, pick up pecans and hickory nuts, fish, roast peanuts, pick blackberries, and fish. Revisiting that year in my life has been both sweet and sad.

A deep rutted road, where we could splash bare feet in the soft dust, led to the old ferry on the Rough River and to the hill where the Hardin home place stood. Our friends lived a few miles up the dusty sometimes muddy road. If I begged long enough and at the right time, I was allowed to go for an hour visit. My marching orders were to be back in an hour and to be sure to run as I passed the Broadman house. I had no problem with the hour limit, but sometimes I wondered if that hour was worth the possibility of being shot to death by a neighbor who lived between us and the Reveletts. Looking back now as an adult who remembers the protective Mom we had, I doubt that I was in much danger, but I always plotted my strategy before hitting the road. A rise in the trail warned me that at the bottom of the hill, I would be in direct range of the gun-toting, porch-sitting, drunken man, Mr. Broadman. If he had a snoot full, he fired a gun. When I was in his sight, I called upon every muscle available in my ten-year-old frame. I laugh now. Even sober, if he were sitting on his porch and looking toward the road, I'm sure all he could have seen was a fog of dust rolling along the road. The scene, I'm sure, a clip from the roadrunner cartoon. Beep! Beep!

I learned another snippet about sex during that

stay in the country. Mom and Dad did not sleep together. Mom usually slept with the girls, Yvonne, Janice and me. One night I awakened to get a drink of water from the kitchen. The path to the water led me through the bedroom where Dad slept. My eyes adjusted to the dimness just enough to see Mom in bed with Dad. There on the floor beside the bed were Mom's step-ins, better known today as panties. Having no clue as to why she would abandon us during the night, I continued to the kitchen. I didn't see Mom or her underwear on my return trip.

My only birthday party was June 3rd, 1955 and it took place in that favorite childhood home, the Schrull Place. I helped Mom wring chickens' necks and peel potatoes as we prepared for the special feast. Dad drove his old truck to the ferry to pick up a few of my girlfriends. I don't remember candles, nor do I remember all those who attended, but I recall receiving a dollar in one envelope. I knew that would cover about twenty recesses when we returned to school. Math was not and is not my strong attribute, but when it comes to buying food, the equation comes easily.

Some neighbor teens came by as we were eating. One boy made the mistake of walking to the table and reaching across to nab him a piece of chicken. I was mortified as Mom slapped his hand and recited the proper table manners in the Hardin household. Those rules included: don't talk with your mouth full, don't reach across others, the table is a place to be seen and not heard, and don't take the last piece of meat until everyone is finished (I don't recall this rule working really well sometimes).

Dad seldom missed when he aimed a gun. A rambunctious cow escaped from a farm in the county. It was destroying fields and gardens, so the farmer spread the word that anyone who could find and destroy the cow could keep it for the meat. When Dad and my brother Eugene drove into the yard with the poor bloody, still, animal, I swore I would not eat anything that looked like that. They delivered the cow to a locker for processing. Dad would go there to pick up what meat we needed. Mom made hamburgers a few nights later. They were considered a treat for us. I had not given the bloody cow another thought. The first bite of a real ground beef burger remains one of the highlights of my cuisine connoisseur life. Even after being told what I was eating, my appetite for fresh ground beef never waned. The expression, eating high off the hog applied to our meals for months as we ate high off the cow.

I ate turtle many times thinking it was chicken. One day as we headed around the road to the garden, Dad spotted a huge turtle crossing our path. He killed it quickly, and since Janice was very little help in the garden anyway, he sent her home with the turtle. Eugene and I laughed as we watched Jaybug gripping that turtle by the tail, tears flowing and struggling down the road to home. Our laughter quieted when we were threatened only once. Returning from the hoeing and picking, we knew Janice had made it home by the wide trail which wiped out most of her bare footprints in the dusty road.

For supper that night we had fried turtle. Dad had to force me to eat that horrible meat which I had enjoyed as chicken for years.

Janice and I bobbed around in the rusty truck bed as Dad bounced from rut to rut up the dirt road which led us beside an old barn and into a sloping green yard at Kronos, Kentucky. Great Aunt Virgie Hunter lived there alone. My Ardoth radar kicked in immediately: new territory to inspect, new people to quiz, nice Sunday for me. I immediately fell in love with that tall, willowy, gray-haired lady who answered the door. She wore a full- length flowered apron, brown socks, and black brogans.

While everyone else shared the usual hellos, hugs, and re-introductions of the kids who had grown up since the last visit, anxious to check out the place, I eased toward an open doorway. In the bedroom, my eyes set immediately upon a tall ornate wooden cabinet. Two bottom doors on the cabinet sported pretty pearl-like knobs. However, the best mystery was the big bugle perched on the top of the cabinet.

Food was not my main interest at that moment, but as most folks did and many still do in Kentucky, we feed company. While the old people sat around the dinner table and reminisced, Janice and I played in the immense front yard. I wanted to live there forever.

Aunt Virgie must have connected with me because she often smiled and winked at my glowing face. When she mentioned that she wished she had a little girl like me, I was elated. Then to my great surprise and utter joy, she asked Mom and Dad if I could spend the week with her. No hesitation from me. After much discussion and plans for what I could wear for a week, Mom relented.

I then just wanted everyone to leave quickly so I could begin my new adventure. My only moment of indecision came as I watched the old truck bounce out of sight around the barn. Before the dust settled, I refocused and just stood smiling up at this wonderful new person in my life.

The first afternoon chore took us to the barn to feed chickens of all sizes and colors. They were yellow, black checkered, white, feather tufted, and all of them pecked, clucked, and sang chicken songs. The fat bottomed ladies would strike a long cawing note while the little yellows peeped out high short chirps. The stately roosters just strutted around growling at everyone. Aunt Virgie put some soft grain on my bare feet so the baby yellows would gently nip and peck my bare skin. Some buried their beaks between my toes to furrow out the food. *So,* I must have thought, *this is what heaven is like.* All I could think about then was that I could do this for a whole week.

Next, we needed to carry in water for the night because Mom had left instructions for Aunt Virgie as to my bathing every night. In the summer, by the time I had played barefoot all day, I was, as Mom said, "rotten." We kids usually took off our shoes in May and only wore them occasionally until September.

I carried a small lard can, while Auntie carried two large water pails. Instead of going to an outdoor faucet, we headed down a well-traveled path toward the woods. I still feel the thrill of our first of many trips to the cool spring by the big tree root. As if by magic, a small stream of water seeped from under a rock and formed a clear mini waterfall which emptied into a bowl shaped rock.

The bucolic scene enamored me until suddenly a tall- legged spider skated and skipped across the water. The only bugs I like are lady bugs. Using my lard bucket, Aunt Virgie began dipping the cool water into her pails as I stood watch for the skipping spider. She offered me a drink from a dipper that hung inside one of her buckets, but all I could picture were those tiny spider toes leaving debris behind for me to drink or a worse scenario of the thing jumping straddle my nose to stare into my petrified eyes. I saw Aunt Virgie's disappointment, and I was very thirsty after our long walk. Peering closely into the clear water, I took a sip. Brave now and still thirsty, I took a gulp of the best water I would taste until fifty-four years later when I drank water in Anchorage, Alaska.

That new world took its toll on my ten-year-old inquisitive body. Exhausted, I sat quietly on the step that led to the bugle room. Aunt Virgie heated water in a kettle on top of an old stove. At the same time, she put supper on the table. I don't remember what food was being served. I just remember two large glasses of sweet milk looming like white towers of torture and knew that one must be for me. I never liked milk. I still can't drink milk. Never wanting to hurt feelings, I tried to form a plan to somehow dispose of what looked like a whole gallon of nasty. I drew on earlier lessons learned and decided to just be honest. She gladly poured the milk back into the pitcher and handed me a glass of cool, delicious, spider free, spring water.

I sat on the step while Aunt Virgie washed my skinny, nude body. As she raised a leg to scrub my rotten feet, a very noisy, elongated, stinky, toot escaped from my mortified frame. The reactions to my action took eons. Auntie's body shook and from her came a sound not unlike the clucking of the old hens we had fed earlier. My reaction was delayed as I tried to figure out whether she was laughing or crying. As she wiped her eyes and blew her nose on her apron, I realized that she was so amused she was doing both. I joined in the fun only to be mortified again as a sput-sput-sput noise sounded from the bottom of the cane bottom chair where Aunt Virgie was seated. By the time we were able to control our laughter, I knew I would love this old lady forever. She pinned someone's underwear on me and wrapped me in a stranger's gown. I scrambled onto the feather bed and remembered nothing until I heard the barn roosters' songs calling for the sun to rise.

In the corner, directly across the room, stood the bugle. The aroma of bacon and coffee and looking forward to another day in this paradise was almost too much for my young mind to comprehend. No TV, no radio, no telephone, no electric, no toys. I didn't miss them because I had none at home. I created my own enjoyment.

As if by magic, my jeans, shirt, and underwear appeared clean and folded on an old rocking chair beside the bed. Looking back, I'm sure Aunt Virgie hand washed my clothes, hung them for the night and pressed them dry with her heavy stove-heated irons.

I politely inhaled breakfast, helped with the dishes, as I had been taught to do, and headed for the bugle. She showed me how to wind a handle on the Victrola, place a record under the needle held there by a heavy arm. Joy, joy, joy! What a joyous feeling streamed through me as I listened to the bugle sing, "The Wreck of Old 97" over and over and over. It was the only record that would play on the machine. I slowed my rhythm and singing as the Victrola wound down. I cranked my arm so much that first day that it was painful to lift the next morning. How in the world did Aunt Virgie listen to a squealing ten- year-old twang out an ancient railroad song hour after hour for seven days?

The chickens, trips to the spring, the old Victrola, great meals, and stories of old times were wonderful, but I did venture outside alone occasionally, as long as I promised to stay in sight. Under the house eave I spotted an empty, rusty rain barrel. At first I just rolled it down the hill in the front yard, across the bottom and then back into the yard at a smaller incline. Having mastered this feat, I decided that it would be more fun to walk the barrel through its paces. After several attempts to climb aboard, I discovered that I could place the barrel near the porch and step onto it with ease. My first few attempts sent me spread eagle onto the hard lawn. By dinner time I had learned to walk atop the barrel, controlling its descent and path with my feet movements. By evening, I mastered my new skills to the point that I could ably walk my ride to any place in the yard, without many mishaps.

One day I proudly fed the chickens by myself. However, my joyous times crumbled when I stepped on a little yellow feather ball. I started making plans to revive him/her, but I quickly realized that it needed new guts to live and new feet to walk again. At first, I waited to be attacked by a thousand angry, grieving chickens. But they were not concerned. My relief became fear. A fear gripped me so hard that I started crying for Mom. I ran screaming toward the house and was met by a very concerned Aunt. After blubbering the news to her, we returned to the barn. I hoped, as we neared the murder scene, that the little mass would be up pecking and chirping with the others. Didn't happen!

We retrieved a shovel from the barn shed and together chose a spot to bury the body. We stacked rocks on top of the tiny grave so the night varmints would not dig it up. Aunt Virgie's long bony fingers swallowed my small hand as we slowly walked home. She smiled, winked, and swore me to secrecy because she knew Mom would be upset.

When Dad's truck lumbered from behind the barn the next Sunday, I was happy and sad. Aunt Virgie and I babbled on forever about the special days we had shared. She told my parents that she hoped we could do this again. We never did. My Mom and Dad parted ways a few months later and life took me in many new directions.

CHAPTER 10

JOURNEY THROUGH PUBERTY

Adolescence is a period of rapid changes. Between the ages of twelve and seventeen, for example, a parent ages as much as twenty years.

--Author Unknown

Students at LHS who qualified were given a chance to work in the lunchroom to pay for their lunches. I qualified. At the time, I was not aware of why I had been chosen for what I thought was a privilege and lots of fun.

All workers had to furnish their own hairnets. I could never find a safe place to store that slippery piece of nylon so I lost many. My usual hiding place was inside the pages of one of my school books. The nets came in three to a package for a nickel. Sometimes I just didn't have the money to buy new nets. If we had no net, they would ask another person who had one to work that day. I found a soft touch in

Mrs. Willis, one of the lunchroom ladies. She stood about 5'2" short so she seemed less imposing than Mrs. Puckett who was a taller, imposing, sweet lady. Mrs. Willis always found a spare net for me. I loved all the lunchroom workers, but these two were my favorites.

I stood proud as I served my fellow students real mashed potatoes, buttery peas, meatloaf and sweets. I have tried all my cooking life to prepare sloppy joes and green peas that taste like those served at LHS.

We were instructed as to how much to put on each plate, but I had my favorite, my little sis, Janice. I knew what she liked best so she received a heaping helping when I served. Some days Janice did not eat with us. I learned by listening, as I still try to do, that many times Mom did not have the money for her to eat, so she had to take her lunch. She didn't like that. I went to Mrs. Willis and asked her if she would let my sister eat on the days I worked instead of me. She turned and walked away. Looking back, I'm sure she turned away because of her emotions. I still had not put the scenarios together and figured out that the poorest were the students chosen to help in the kitchen.

Most of the time, we just washed dishes. Jean, my good friend and neighbor, worked with me many times. What a treat for me to turn on a faucet and out came hot water to wash the many dishes. One day as I washed and she rinsed, she almost fainted as I handed her an electric mixer which I had doused in the soapy water and scrubbed diligently. Since I was not used to electrical appliances, I had no clue about washing them. Jean hurriedly dried the mixer and placed it on a nearby table. She later told me why I should not have immersed it in water. I don't recall worrying about it, but again, I had no knowledge of the power of electricity.

The next day, with hair net in hand, I headed down to the basement five minutes before the lunch bell rang. Excitement reigned supreme in that tiny kitchen at LHS. A major nasty smell greeted me as I entered the room. All the cooks seemed to be jabbering at the same time. Jean had arrived early and had pieced the rambling conversations together. Mrs. Willis had plugged in the very clean mixer in order to whip the cornbread batter. When the sizzling sound ceased, black smoke spewed out of every hole in the appliance. I guess she finished stirring the meal mixture the old time way, with a fork or whisk. After the initial shock, no pun intended, the cooks realized this was their chance to get a big, modern bowl mixer. Jean warned me not to say a word. Jean saved me many times as we grew up. I really wanted to let the ladies know that I was happy to make one of their wishes come true, but they never knew.

Puberty presented challenges to my body and mind that I didn't understand. The combination of my age, twelve, and a dodge ball game, one day changed my competitive nature and my attitude for life.

This is another time that I find no comic relief for a crisis in my childhood.

I knew I should never make fun of people. I knew that I should not succumb to peer pressure. I knew! But this day the devil tap danced loudly on my shoulder.

Dodge ball, basketball, softball, foot racing, and

any other game, which provided a chance to compete and have fun, appealed to the tomboy in me. Our class engaged in a heated, take'm-down dodge ball game. The successful catches that burned my hands and chest didn't faze me because it meant that I remained in the game. The hits on my body that sat me on the sideline hurt two ways. Some girls tried to hide behind the "brave." Sometimes a girl would make a deal with one of the competitors to hit her and then she could sit until another game. I never thought I would someday use this ruse so that I could avoid playing.

Mildred Ann was a sweet, somewhat fragile classmate who played for the opposing team that day. The game became quite rough, so the teachers yelled warnings reminding us of the rules of the game. The other team was winning. Someone on my team noticed that Mildred had worn different colored socks. The different shades were barely noticeable but provided fodder for poking fun and maybe disrupting the opposition's concentration.   Students jeered at Mildred who was one of the most popular and nice students in our school. I joined in. Yes, I don't remember anything I said, but I know my words were wrong and hurtful. She finally cried and left the game. Only then did my conscience kick in. I wanted to go to her to comfort her, but I knew the others would consider me a traitor. I planned to catch her away from my other friends and tell her how sorry I felt, but that was the last time I saw Mildred alive.

She did not attend school for the next few days, and we heard that she was seriously ill. Most families had no phones, so the backyard fence served as our communication medium. One evening as Mom removed clothes from the line, a neighbor came over to bring bad news. Mildred Ann had died. The sickness in my heart overwhelmed me. I went to bed early and mentally reviewed the last day I had seen my friend. Not wanting to tell Mom or anyone, I just silently cried and started taking the blame for her death. I thought I remembered maybe hitting her with the ball that day. I wondered if I had hit her in a place which caused her death.

Mom insisted I go to school. The whole day moved in slow motion. I heard only that it was something in her brain that caused her death. Sometimes I would just stare toward her empty space and cry. I was not alone in my grief; I just had a secret, painful heart that I never wanted to reveal. I should say that these are the memories I wish I had lost through the sieve, but I learned so many lessons in those days that I should be glad they remain a part of me.

I do not recall the funeral.

A few days after the funeral, I became ill. Mom said I probably had the flu which was ravaging the town. This time though Mom seemed more concerned than usual. She insisted on keeping a close eye on my temperature. Finally, I began to recover. Mom's statement will forever be with me. She said, "I have been so worried that you could become seriously ill since you had the same flu which Mildred died from." I asked Mom to repeat what she had said. Instead of Mildred's death occurring because of an injury, she had died from complications of the flu. I guess looking back, Mom must have thought I had lost my mind. Although still weak, I jumped up and gave her a hug.

I learned to share my worries with Mom and ask

questions. I learned why it is not only hurtful to make fun of someone but also painful to me. I learned that peer pressure is easy to give in to.

The dodge ball games became a real challenge for me, not because of the competition, but because I did not want to participate. I called in some favors and many times took the hit so that I could leave the game early.

I "came around" as Mom used to say, when I became a teen. To show how little I knew about the female curse, I must tell you of another time my good pal Jean rescued me. I had passed the white metal box hanging on the wall in the girls' restroom many times. I had seen girls put in a nickel, turn a knob, and collect a small container. Standing beside the box one day waiting for Jean to come out of a stall, I began to spell "KOTEX" aloud.

After my second or third spelling, Jean yelled, "Shut up, Ardoth." She immerged from her stall red faced and scolded me soundly. She asked me if I knew what the box contained. Of course, I didn't. After giving me an "I don't believe it" stare, she told me to ask Mom. I did not.

One day I awakened to find spots in my underwear. Concerned, I tried to remember how I had injured myself while playing my usual tomboy games. After exhausting all probably scenarios, I told Mom. She led me to a closet where a large box full of, what I thought were, humongous bandages lay stuffed in a back corner. Mom handed me one that must have been a one-size-fits-all. Then she explained that I needed to put this wad of white inside my panties. I probably weighed all of 90 lbs. and stood about five feet short.

With a very full crotch, I headed to school. I spent the rest of my day picturing everyone staring at my new bulge. The next morning, I went to the dreaded closet and retrieved another pad. I thought, what a miserable thing to happen. After about ten days of adjusting, learning a new walk, and checking to make sure I had not lost my protection, Mom told me that this great burden only occurred once a month. Oh, what a relief.

Ardoth Hardin Wilkerson

CHAPTER 11

YVONNE

Between sisters, often, the child's cry never dies down, "Never leave me," it says; "do not abandon me."

--Louise Bernikow

The Hardin union produced its first little girl December 26th, 1940. Dr. Deweese advised Mom and Dad to institutionalize Yvonne. Of course, they would not, so she became our Vonnie; she remained a blessing and a challenge to all of us. Her mental problems were diagnosed by one doctor as Down syndrome, another simply said that she came from an old egg and referred to her as a Mongoloid. In her later years doctors just called her mentally challenged.

There were no programs to aid those needy, special people. By the time the programs came into existence, Mom had developed a daily routine with Yvonne, and she would not trust others with her baby girl. I know Yvonne would have accomplished so much had she been able to attend programs that are available today, but she was always loved and taken care of by Mom and the family.

Although she was four years older than I, she became my baby sister. She never progressed past the mentality of a three-year-old. Think how absolutely special it would be to live the innocent life of a three-year-old. Of course, her body changed as she grew into adulthood. She experienced puberty, menopause, and probably other maladies which affect the woman world.

Yvonne's disability caused her to withdraw from others many times and her anger became scary to us when she would rip at her clothes and scream or cry loudly. Almost daily, Mom repaired her simple homemade dresses. At an early age I learned to sew; many times I helped Mom mend the damaged clothing. Mostly, Yvonne remained quiet and found her joy in playing with dolls. Mom would not allow her to use scissors. When we gave her scraps of material so she could fashion clothes for her dollies, she easily tore that cloth into tiny underwear, skirts and dresses. I only wish I had kept some of those sweet little outfits to show folks what a talent she had.

I don't recall Vonnie ever being bathed in a tub until she lived in a nursing home. She was not agile and became excited quickly and unexpectedly. Sometimes I helped Mom bathe her from head to toe with a pan of water or while she stood at a sink. She would lean her head over to have her hair washed, but she didn't like that part so we had to find her in the right mood and then hurry. I sneaked one time and put her in a tub. Lordy, I had the bejebbies scared out of me. She started slipping when she placed her first foot in the tub. Vonnie was always large and at that time probably weighed 200 pounds. Imagine struggling with a 200 pound, scared three-year-old. She finally sat down so hard that a tsunami swept over the side of the tub. I convinced her to just sit still while I sopped up the water. I scrubbed her back and used the shower hose to wash her hair squeaky clean. All the time I wondered how in the world I could get her out. There was nothing for her to grasp except the sides of the slippery tub. I tried to get her to her knees. Didn't happen! Then we got tickled. I finally climbed into the tub behind her and managed to push as she pushed. Never again! Moms know their children best.

Vonnie was a sweet gift from God. Her vocabulary was foreign to everyone except the family. She loved Santa. To her, Santa was Deller, Deller. Always wanting a doll, she cradled her arms and rocked left to right and asked for a garley. She loved chicken and requested jarnie for supper often. She could say yes, no, mama, and baby. Eugene was her jeje. She spoke Oliver's name very well. She called Janice and me Gordy, and Tommy was named Guy. And visitors were also Gordy most of the time. She could never say my name, but a year before she passed, I sat with her for over an hour and we practiced. She loved to laugh. She didn't tire in that whole hour, but we would get so tickled at her attempts to say Ardoth. When she finally said my name plainly, I cried as she laughed and patted my head.

My Dad used colorful language. Vonnie picked up a few of his words that she put to good use when she was angry or hurting. Her favorite rebellious words were, damit batechimgoatie. Of course, the word that came out plainly was damit.

Vonnie needed her gallbladder removed. Her doctor requested an around-the-clock nurse, who stayed with her even when the family visited. After her surgery, which was the radical full incision type, the nurse and I waited for her to come out of the anesthesia. Slowly she opened her eyes. I stood on one side of her bed while the nurse, a petite little gal, stood on the other side. Vonnie placed her hand on her stomach, squinted, and distinctly yelled, damit batechimgoatie. I just turned red and smiled. I calmed her as the wide-eyed nurse gave her an injection. Then Vonnie swung her legs to the side of the bed and headed to the bathroom. We grabbed her IV pole and hurried with her. She peed and evidently feeling the morphine, smiled a big ole Vonnie smile. The doctor worried that she would have trouble urinating. Didn't happen! We took her home two days early because she seemed to not understand that she was recovering from a major surgery.

In their later years, she and Mom stayed in an assisted living home. Vonnie bloomed. During our visits she expressed her excitement with her new environment by using her unique hand and verbal communications. Mom's health failed first, and she was moved to a skilled care home. Vonnie lived at Rosedale among friends and great caring nurses, who were her extended family, until her death.

Ardoth and Vonnie

Ardoth Hardin Wilkerson

CHAPTER 12

HOMETOWN

We all have hometown appetites. Every other person is a bundle of longing for the simplicities of good taste once enjoyed on the farm or in his or her hometown.

--Clementine Paddleford

A hometown is defined as a city or town where someone is born or raised. What a simple definition for such an important community which took on the task of trying to channel my youthful energy toward a fulfilled Christian life. Many firsts for me took place in my hometown of Livermore, Kentucky.

My adventures, while roaming the streets and sidewalks of Livermore, sometimes led me to the banks of Green River which meanders from Lincoln County, Kentucky, through the great Mammoth Cave, and allows Rough River to join it just below the famous highway 431 bridge. It is the only bridge in the world that crosses two rivers and carries travelers from one county to another county and then back into the first county. I had no idea that bridge is unique. I just knew that there was a great bluegill hole beside one of its giant columns, our first home was at the foot of the bridge, and many evenings I watched Bert Simpson climb down a metal ladder to turn on the bridge lights.

No one appointed me "little miss fix it" but somehow my environment shaped my psyche into believing there is a solution to most problems, and it is my job to seek those solutions, especially if I have caused the problem in the first place. We always had clothes to wear, food each meal, and a clean home. I had plenty of hints as to the difficult times my parents had in providing those essentials. Looking back, I now realize that our clothes were not fancy, our shoes were completely used up before we had new ones, and that food existed back then with names like baked Alaska and lobster bisque. I also realize that the blackberry cobblers and fried catfish fiddlers were just as delicious and nourishing as the classy dishes we had never known about.

I always enjoyed trips to town because that always gave me more territory to either conquer or divide. Mom needed sugar which was purchased by the pound. I cautiously crossed 431, ran down the hill between the Lloyd and Thornberry's homes and then skipped my way through the alley to Hill Street. Once on the sidewalk, I began flipping my quarter high, catching it and guessing heads or tails as I slapped it onto my skinny, freckled arm.

In front of Atherton's grocery, a wide menacing

square hole loomed in the sidewalk. I had never walked on it and only occasionally peered down through the iron grating with wonder as to why it even existed. I rounded the store corner, flipped my coin and missed. It rolled quickly toward the slots in the sidewalk as if being sucked into it by some invisible force.

Twenty-five cents gone! I eased to the edge of the dark precipice. There nestled among the candy wrappers, gum wads, leaves, sticks and other unidentifiable debris, Mom's quarter starkly stared back at me. I had to fix this one. I knew that quarter would buy a large bag of sugar, and I knew that I would have to tell the truth to Mom about my mishap.

I never entertained the idea of poking around in that mass of nasty to retrieve my coin. I did discover, with further inspection, that the hole seemed to be connected to Atherton's store. I had no vision of my crawling through that underground, dark cave, but I hoped the folks inside may have a way of sucking the precious money out, just as it had been sucked in. I eased through the squeaky, heavy door. Two tall imposing men stood behind a long counter. Instead of my bravado carrying me through the scene I had envisioned of telling them that their sidewalk hole had swallowed my money, I began to sob loudly. I'm sure one of the gentlemen inquired as to my problem. I blubbered out the whole story quickly. I'm sure they smiled as to my request for someone to please retrieve Mom's money. One gentleman reached in a cash register and handed me a quarter. Relief was not a word with a strong enough meaning to describe how I felt. After a smile and a thank you, I took the quarter, left the store and continued down the street to Scott's grocery to purchase the sugar.

When I purchased the sugar that time, I asked for the full quarter's worth. Usually, I bought twenty-four cents worth of sugar and Kits which were two packages for a penny. I usually bought peanut and plain. I now wonder how in the world Barney Scott weighed that sugar so closely as to have a penny left for me.

Jean Crowe, my pal from P Ridge, and I usually walked home from school together. One day as we climbed the hill beside Mrs. Lloyd's, I noticed a large coin lying in the grass that had been recently burned. Highway 431 often had small burns on the roadside when people threw out cigarettes. I retrieved the fifty-cent piece. We continued to search the slope and found several more scorched coins. Elated, we headed for home. Mom was happy, but unsure as to whether we should keep the money. Dad solved the wonder quickly. He returned with me to the scene where we found only one more coin. We will never know where this windfall came from, but Dad said it sure came in handy.

My first attempt at entrepreneurship began when I talked Mom into allowing me to sell Grit papers, Cloverine salve, and punch boards. I quickly established a few regular customers. As an adult looking back on my business endeavors, I wonder how many of my customers really needed my products or just saw a barefoot, towhead Hardin, trying to make money.

I carried a canvas bag over my shoulder, after tying a knot in the long strap so it would not drag the ground. If I had extra papers, I would just knock on doors until I had sold all the news.

An unusual structure occupied the small corner of Third and Main streets. Behind the building stood a large house. I climbed a few steps to the home, pecked on the door and sold a Grit to an elderly gentleman. I then went back to the sidewalk, around the corner, knocked on a door to hopefully sell another paper. The same man came to the door, paper still in hand. Red faced, I just smiled my smile. He smiled as I scurried back to the sidewalk. His home bordered two streets- one on each side if the little corner structure.

Imagine allowing a nine-year-old to peddle salve and newspapers door to door today.

My later job after selling Grit papers and Cloverine salve was sitting with an elderly neighbor who paid fifty cents each night. We ate the same thing each night unless I took leftovers from home. I prepared us an old fashion loaf sandwich. Mrs. Jessie usually gave half of hers to her dog. We talked every night until we fell asleep. I decided to maybe become a caregiver or nurse when I grew up.

Another money mystery occurred after we had moved into town. I loved to play in the rain. I especially enjoyed going out barefoot after a downpour to play in the ditches and pools of water. As I waded in the swift ankle deep water in front of our home one day, I leaned down to peer into a large culvert. A mound of something shiny caught my eye. Of course, I had to inspect further. There, as if the sky had rained money, stood a pile of what looked like newly minted pennies.

Mom came out to confirm my find. We carried a

little bucket of pennies into the house. When I went to the store for us in the next few days, I paid with pennies. Of course, Mom allowed me to buy a few Kits too.

I never solved the money mysteries. I also never solved the mystery which came in the mail for weeks after Mom had been very ill and unable to go door to door to sell Fashion Frocks.

As Mom opened the mail one day, she seemed puzzled. She removed a five dollar bill from the plain envelope with no return address. She questioned me to be certain that I had been handed the mail by the post people. She inspected the address to see if she may recognize the hand writing. I don't know the exact value of five dollars in 1960, but I know that in 1962, Tommy and I bought a week's supply of groceries for two with that amount.

One week from that day, another envelope arrived with another bill inside. Mom splurged that night and bought us a can of pork with a little pouch of bar-b-cue sauce in the middle.

My days' thoughts revolved around that post office mystery. I told no one. I just hurried to retrieve the mail daily. I dreamed about Mom maybe opening an envelope with one hundred dollars in it. I began looking at folks in church, school and on the street differently. Searching faces was not new to me, searching with a mission was new. If a teacher looked at me a little differently, I wondered. When someone smiled at me in church, I wondered if that was an, "I'm the one smile."

Where in my young mind were the thoughts that someone may feel sorry for us because we were in need? Didn't happen! I just wanted someone to hug and to thank.

I cannot recall how long the envelopes continued to arrive. I know they came for many weeks until Mom fully recovered. That also remained an unsolved mystery. The precious gifts brought us more than food for our family. Even though we had no idea as to the giver, I felt closer to more people in our community as I imagined any one of them as our benefactor.

Although Livermore youngsters did not fear the day or night streets, there were two incidents which impacted my life and left a secret fear in me.

Two men, who today would be called pedophiles, exposed their sick minds by invading my youthful innocent world. Both are dead now. At the age of twelve, a local, well-known resident found the two of us alone. He told me he had something special in his hands to show me. As I approached him, he suddenly grabbed my arm and pulled me roughly against him. I had no notion as to what his intentions were; I just knew I didn't like the scene. He then cupped my face in his rough hand and began kissing me and literally slobbering and moaning. Now, my fear turned to anger. I jerked at his arm and started to scream. He them placed his hand across my mouth and in a horrible, husky voice warned me not to tell anyone or I would be in lots of trouble.

I ran straight home to tell Mom. I will forever remember Mom's anger and concern when I finished my story. She asked me if I had told her everything that had happened and then literally flew out the door. Mom returned later, not a bit calmer, and told me that I would never have to worry about that nasty person bothering me again. Mom also asked me not to tell anyone, especially Dad, who would probably kill the man and go to jail. Never, in my uninformed mind, did I realize what that man wanted or what could have happened to me. Until he died, this sick man, lived among the regular folks in Livermore, and I lived with my secret.

At the age of thirteen, I often switched off oil pumps for Dad. The pump houses were always dark. I knew the location of the switches so I usually just reached in to turn off the pump. This evening a man lurked in the shadowy corner of the building. He grabbed my arm and an earlier scene repeated itself. This time I was a stronger adversary. I didn't just attempt to do harm to that nasty old, old man, I did. I flailed away at his face with my fists, kicked him, and finally ran home, again. I told my story, again, with the same reactions from Mom.

I never learned how Mom handled the first situation, but in reflection I figure she threatened to tell his wife and his parents. She did tell me how she had settled the new one. She went to the man and in front of his wife she shared the incident. He denied it until he realized his wife knew the time frame, knew he was gone from home then, and he had come home with a bloody ear. Both begged Mom not to tell Dad.

Did I grow up in a perfect little country town that had no deviates in its citizenry? No, has anyone had that privilege? I grew up in a small city full of folks who lived in a mostly loving, caring, environment. They bought my Grit papers, Cloverine salve, and tolerated my pestering to sell my punch boards. LHS provided quality teachers and a quality education for me. After the sad loss of our family members, we were not ostracized; we were embraced by most of the community. Sundays spent in the Livermore Missionary Baptist church laid a Christian foundation for my future. I married and moved across the river to Island, but Livermore will always be my hometown.

Ardoth Hardin, 1960, age 15

Howard Thomas Wilkerson, 1960, age 18

CHAPTER 13

CONCEPTION, MARRIAGE, LOVE

Anything I have ever done that ultimately was worthwhile... initially scared me to death.

--Betty Bender

Following eighth-grade graduation, we simply moved next door to the high school section of LHS.

Our neighboring town across Green River, known as Island, had no high school. Upon graduation they were assigned to either Sacramento High School or LHS. For most of our incoming freshmen, these transfers meant there would be more fish in the sea. For me, I really didn't consider it a momentous happening. The first few days of ninth grade were so exciting and confusing that I took very little notice of the transfers.

Most of the upperclassmen looked at us as invading peons. While many of my friends scoped out the newcomers, my focus remained on the new teachers and new curriculum. I have never understood why the traditional time frame of female maturity evaded me. While other thirteen and fourteen-year-old girls embraced puberty and learned to enjoy the company of the opposite sex, I remained devoted to sports, reading, cooking, and studying.

But, by mid-semester, I dove right into that hormonal sea of teens and enjoyed the life of poodle skirts, black and white oxfords, penny loafers, nickel jukebox tunes, fountain cokes, rock and roll, band trips, flirting, church, drag racing during lunch, and red lipstick.

First, I bought a pointed bra. The girls who were "in the know," wore v neck sweaters and necklaces that accentuated the usually small cleavage between the points. I learned to tilt my shoulders slightly backwards so I didn't look as if I were aimed downhill as I walked.

I attempted to shave the few blonde hairs from my legs and underarms. The only razor in our house was a double edged type. I placed the blade in and screwed on the top plate. The fine hairs would not come off. They wanted to lie limp on my skin and hang on. I decided to open the top plate a little on the razor to get more traction. It took three weeks for the scabs to fall off the front of my bony shin.

The boys noticed my dimples, thus I laughed often. Listening to the girls talk about their good times with the boys became a highlight for my day. One friend bragged about the mosquito bites she had on her butt after a date with her boyfriend. I had no notion as to why everyone thought that to be so funny.

A tall, skinny Island boy and his friend checked out

the girls one day. Walking behind me in the hallway, Tommy Wilkerson told his friend that he planned to get better acquainted with that little Hardin girl. The friend acted quickly and asked me for a date. His friend had no car or license, so Tommy transported us around on dates occasionally. The only boy/girl interaction I had had before was walking to Kokomo's for a coke or to night church. One boy who was visiting a family friend had introduced me to French kissing. His name happened to be Tommy also. My first romance lasted only a short time.

Tommy Wilkerson and I began dating seriously in June of 1960. I think "seriously" meant that we saw only each other.

Mom continued to tell me to be good when I was with a boy. I never questioned her as to what she thought I may do that was not good except one time I do remember becoming belligerent when leaving for a date with Tommy. When Mom reminded us to be good, I asked her if she thought we were going to rob a bank or something. Tommy knew what Mom was alluding to. But, Tommy and I were both fully into the puppy love stage of our relationship.

We learned together about sex and love. The sex came first, and I am not sure when the real love phase entered my life. The only time I have experienced love at first sight was when my eyes set upon my children and grandchildren.

I was not happy with the sex part of our relationship because it seemed to this fifteen-year-old such a silly and unnatural action. Hindsight kicked in though, and I finally figured out things like the pigpen and thicket visits. That really bummed me out. How in the world could my parents want to do that "thing"?

In my mind, only married people had children. Remember folks, I always needed to put the parts of life's puzzles together after the fact and then digest the meaning of what had happened. Tommy asked me often if I had had my monthly. I thought he asked because we would not be so close during those times.

When I skipped two months, he became concerned. He explained that we should go to see Dr. Scott for a pregnancy test. The emotions that engulfed me were such a mixture of confusion, wonderment, and fear. I went home that night and tried to figure out why I was having a baby before being married. I did figure that our silly sex had caused it, and I figured that this was my part of not being good.

Dr. Scott began to assemble needles and other horrible gadgets to draw our blood. I leaped from the table to inform him that I would not be stuck with that needle. Doc finally gave me the ultimatum: no blood test, no marriage. I am sure Tommy had figured out by now that his work as a husband and father may include two children, one fifteen and one newborn. With the blood test drama over, he continued to guide me through the days that were just a blur of secret looks and whispered words. Confirmation came in a few days. My first gynecological examination followed. Doc's whole conversation was, "You are about three months along."

Tommy was an eighteen-year-old senior at LHS; I was a fifteen-year-old sophomore. My plans were to be a doctor, not ever marry, and to have no children.

His plans were to someday secure a good paying job, marry and have five children. Well, one of our plans was about to get off to an early start.

I thought I had no control over the happenings and no one to ask for advice. Feeling that I had not listened to Mom's advice and knowing she would be afraid for me, I did not tell her. We found our champion in Tommy's Mother. She answered my numerous questions and made me the sweetest blue flowered wedding dress, size 5. She also advised us to tell my parents. Didn't happen!

Tommy continued to do, as many would say, the right thing. He had an after school job. He purchased a set of wedding rings from Zale's Jeweler then picked out a baby blue negligee for our honeymoon. The events rolled by so quickly that I just barely had time to consider my future. I lay in bed the night before our planned wedding and suddenly realized that it may be the last night I would spend with my family. I missed them, before I had even gone. Now I thought, *how was I to become a doctor? No more band, no more glee club, no more cruising to Calhoun with the gang.* My doubts began to scare me, but I also realized that the little body in my body belonged to Tommy and to me. Whether a person wants to or not, taking responsibility for her mistakes remains the most important decision she can make.

January 3rd, 1961, I left home as if to attend another school day. We took a forged marriage license to a justice of peace in Island, Kentucky. There he performed a double wedding. Tommy's sister, Etta Mae, married her fiancé Willard Long. They witnessed our marriage, and we witnessed their marriage.

Returning home to face Mom was one of the saddest things I have ever done. I had been raised to be honest, so the previous weeks had taken their toll on my conscience. I can only imagine her fear and pain when we told her the news. She insisted that I would not leave with Tommy. She insisted that we could raise the baby together as a family. I agreed. I'm sure Tommy must have been weak-kneed at this point. He took one arm and Mom took the other. For an instant, I worried about my safety. Tommy won the pulling match. We quickly stumbled to Willard's waiting vehicle.

Mom then went next door to phone the county attorney who knew our family and the Wilkerson family. He advised Mom to let us give our marriage a try. Mom called Dad. He immediately went to Mom to comfort her and also advised her to let us give it a try.

We four newlyweds were not privy to this knowledge, thus we spent the next few miles looking for the red light behind us. I had no idea that we had done anything illegal. Willard's vehicle broke down before we made it to our Louisville destination. I wasn't that upset because by that time I was ready to go home.

I donned my sweet blue negligee that night in a motel room in Hartford, Kentucky at the Mototel. No, Mototel is not a misspelling.

The next day we returned to Tommy's Island home. He walked to the front of the flaming fireplace, reached in his pocket to take out a quarter, the money we had remaining to start out our married life and prepare to raise a child.

My pregnancy went fairly smoothly except for the early sickness and my huge weight gain. I ate everything edible. Tommy was amazed at my appetite but tried to keep me happy by bringing me candy and other things that I craved daily. Once he reached into his pocket and presented me with what I thought was a coconut square. I chomped down. It didn't have much taste. He began to chuckle. Seems he had picked up a dog treat from a box at Dad's house. I cried and cried. He apologized and apologized. I told him he may have harmed our unborn child. My goodness, we were two children having a child.

July 14th, 1961, Mom and my husband of six months sat in the tiny waiting room at McLean County Hospital. Dad stayed with Vonnie so Mom could be there for the birth of her first grandchild. Now, if anyone expects me to ooh and ahh over the beautiful experience of giving birth, don't. I had never felt such pain in my life. I had never been so scared in my life.

No family member was allowed in the labor room or delivery room. The nurse told me to stop yelling because people could hear me all over the hospital, like I really cared. Tom Jr.'s head crowned before Doctor Scott arrived to block me and deliver him. If Tommy had been in that labor room, I would have punched him out. I did tell him after the delivery that there would be no more sex in our marriage. Howard Thomas Wilkerson Jr. weighed 7 pounds and 9 ounces. Instead of the 99 pounds I had weighed at conception, I weighed 148.

No one told me about after pains, so when by block wore off and my pain started again, I pushed the nurse button to tell her that another baby was on the way.

Dad carried Tom Jr. around town to the pool rooms and the grocery stores to proudly show off his first grandchild. I felt humble and happy that Dad accepted our situation for what it was: two inexperienced teens giving in to hormonal urges.

We did have sex again. A long-toed 9 pound 7 ounce Rodney Lynn Wilkerson screamed his way into our lives November 2nd, 1964.

Our double wedding. January 3, 1961. L to R, Willard Long, Etta Wilkerson Long, Tommy Wilkerson, Ardoth Hardin Wilkerson

CHAPTER 14

AUNT ZEULA

Only an Aunt can give us hugs like a mother, can keep secrets like a sister, and share love like a friend.

--Spanish Proverb

Mom's sister, Aunt Zeula, served as my second Mother. She and Uncle Tom had no children, so I became their surrogate daughter. Aunt Zeula recalled standing behind a door and hearing adults planning to send her and her siblings to an orphanage. She vowed to never have children that she could not raise. She never faced that challenge because she and Uncle Tom were involved in a serious auto accident. They were never able to conceive so she loved on every child she knew.

Their lives were so calm and peaceful compared to the ever eventful lives of my large family. I never missed an opportunity to stop by on my way to or from town.

They had a telephone, bathroom, electricity, television, and icy cold Cokes in 6.5 ounce glass bottles.

A starched white doily cradled the phone which perched on a telephone chair covered in red, white and blue satin stripes. My fascination with the telephone began the first time I laid eyes on it. I watched as Uncle Tom or Aunt Zeula spoke to the unknown. When I could catch Aunt Zeula busy in the kitchen, I always investigated the apparatus. The receiver was so heavy that I had to lift it with both hands. Just listening to the buzzing sound was a treat. I placed my fingers in the holes over the numbers, but I never conjured up enough nerve to spin the dialer. One day, I eased the receiver from its cradle, and a voice jumped from the earpiece. "Hello, hello, Zeula?"

I quickly dropped the receiver and hurried to another chair. Immediately, the phone began to ring. I always enjoyed watching Aunt Zeula slowly lift the mouthpiece to say hello. "No, I didn't hang up on you. My phone has not rung," she said. Silence! "Maybe you need to have your phone fixed." She spoke for a few minutes to the caller then returned to her chores in the kitchen.

Their bathroom held a special fascination for me. It had everything our outside two-holer lacked. I walked on freshly waxed linoleum and little fluffy throw rugs. I inhaled deeply to enjoy the sweet powder aroma and always put my face on the soft pastel towels hanging from various wall racks. Watching the water spiral down the commode became boring after I started to school and used the commodes daily.

On one nosy trip to the bathroom, I noticed a new round container setting on the back of the sink. As usual, I needed to know. So I tried on tip-toe to reach the object of my curiosity. Mom, Yvonne, and Aunt Zeula were visiting in the living room. I sneaked by the door to retrieve a little cane-bottomed chair to use as a booster. I stretched my bony arm to the point that I could touch my prize. Suddenly, the chair shot out from under my naked feet and as I fell, I took the little covered bowl with me. Blue liquid ran down the sides of the sink, but the most frightening part was that someone's gums and teeth lay on the floor staring at me.

"Ardoth, what are you doing in there?" Mom yelled.

My answer was something like, "Nothing, just slipped on the floor."

Mom insisted that I come out of there immediately. Grabbing a towel, I hurriedly wiped at the blue mess. I knew I must put those horrible things back into their hiding place. Not wanting to touch them, I gingerly picked them up with the towel. Having repaired most of the damage and knowing one more minute would bring Mom, I scooped up the chair and headed to the corner of the dining room. A sharp pain in my foot brought me to a quick halt. I sat down, turned my barefoot over to discover a very white tooth stuck between two toes. I grabbed it, stuck it in my pocket and continued my escape.

I never heard from that incident so I have no idea how the mess was explained away. Knowing my sweet Aunt Zeula as well as I do, she probably covered for me.

I was eleven years old before we had electricity or a bathroom and twelve before we had a television. But, I never had those icy cold Cokes in my home until I married.

After Uncle Tom's passing, my husband, boys and I tried to spend time with her since she had never been alone. Her spiritual life was an example that anyone should follow. I have always known that she would see Jesus when she left us. My sons often lovingly remember her sweetness and caring nature. In her later years, Aunt Zeula unintentionally provided us with excitement as we shopped together and spent time as a family.

Once, as she waited for me to check out at a store, she became tired and decided to sit on a box across the aisle from us. I heard a commotion. There sprawled between the sides of an empty toilet tissue box lay my sweet Aunt Zeula, her purse arm gripping one side as she pushed with her other arm to extract her old body from the trap. I wanted to run, but I didn't. I hurried to her aid before her predicament revealed her very granny step-ins. I so appreciated the assistance of strangers. Some just stood and smiled. I'm sure this provided story time that night for many.

Tom Jr. recalls the time we stood in line at Wal-Mart one Christmas season. Aunt Zeula looked back from the checkout isle and spotted some candy hanging from a pegboard. Tom Jr. stood next to the candy, so in her sometimes loud voice, she asked Tom to hand her two packages of "nigger toes."

Tom Jr. stiffened as if he had stuck his finger in a light socket and then turned red from ear to ear. He looked at me for relief. All I could do was hold my stomach tight, tighten my lips to hold the laughter and pluck two bags of chocolate drops from the shelf. I avoided even a slight glance toward Jr. I could only imagine the whirlwind in his brain. He knew his great aunt as a person who would never be prejudice or want to hurt anyone with a racial word. Tom Jr. had black friends and had been taught to respect anyone for who that person was, not the color of the skin.

The black folks who lived in our little town resided on P Ridge which was directly behind our home at the foot of the 431 bridge. They weaved in and out of our lives as t part of the citizenry only they had dark skin. Many of the black folks referred to themselves using the name "nigger" as we may use Mr. or Mrs. A black friend of ours was named Lizzie. When Lizzie came to our door, she always yelled, "Grace, it's nigger Lizzie." I had no idea that the word had any derogatory meaning, and looking back on those years, I don't think our black friends in Livermore, Kentucky felt the anger or hurt feelings toward the use of the word. Maybe it was just innocence of youth. But I just love the notion.

My first encounter with prejudice came when I was fifteen years old and traveled on a big Greyhound from Livermore to Pensacola, Florida. I finally noticed that all the black folks who boarded went directly to the back of the bus. They passed up many empty seats and never smiled back even when I tried to smile at them. My feelings grow raw when I think of anyone attempting to make a fellow human being feel inferior because of skin color. That is one of many lessons I learned from my parents and Aunt Zeula.

Ardoth Hardin Wilkerson

CHAPTER 15

WORKING DAZE

You are never too old to set another goal or to dream another dream.

--C.S. Lewis

A young lady asked me what had been the toughest part of marrying so young. Tough is another one of those words that doesn't reflect the many challenges Tommy and I faced. We struggled emotionally, financially, and physically. There is no way I can glamorize our marriage. Yes, we have celebrated fifty years of marriage. But, we celebrated great times, our victories, and survival of the rough, painful times.

As my figure changed to accommodate our baby, I watched Tommy go off to school to continue life in the educational environment that I loved and he hated. We both agreed that he must get his diploma. In 1961, in McLean County, there were no fifteen or even eighteen- year-old pregnant girls, married or otherwise, gracing the halls of MCHS. If I could have a do-over, I would have been the first. I stayed home to cook, visit Mom and Dad, and do Tommy's homework while he worked at the local garage each night and weekends. His grades actually improved!

I missed the proms, the ball games, the classes, the teachers, the learning, the graduations, and my friends. My new life was not just new but scary. Suddenly, I had to take charge of the, who, what, where, when and how's in my life. When did I clean my home? What did I cook? How did I keep from being jealous of Tommy? Where did I channel my resentment? It took years to understand that my attitude toward each challenge would dictate the outcome.

Then at the age of seventeen, I began working as a housekeeper at our new McLean County Hospital. I lied about my age. After a few weeks I trained as a nurse's aide. In the sixties, the aide performed many of the duties that LPN's perform today. Every nurse should write a book.

The first female I catheterized was a girl I knew well. I contaminated the first sterile pack, which I am sure did not comfort the patient. After some gentle probing, I retrieved a very small sample. She told me she had recently urinated. My hands were shaking as I headed to the lab with the specimen. I was glad the vial was covered. By the time I reached the lab, I was crying. "Mrs. Nall, I could just get this little bit out of her! Do you think I used the right hole?"

Sweet Mrs. Nall just laid her head on her desk and laughed. I did have enough urine. I did use the correct procedure. I did learn many things from Mrs. Nall.

At the age of eighteen, I experienced by sight what I had experienced at the birth of my first son. I assisted the doctor in the delivery of a baby boy. My hands shook as I tied the doctor's gown. It fell off as he leaned over. Oops! I handed him instruments and tried to view every step he took to coax the baby out of its comfortable surroundings. I remained very engrossed in the amazing happening until he asked the nurse for forceps. He placed the vise-like instrument on that tiny head, propped his foot on the bottom of the gurney and pulled. Lordy! I thought I would surly faint. I knew I would if that baby's head flew off as I envisioned. My mouth is so many times my enemy. I yelled, "Don't pull its head off."

Oh my, what must that mother have thought had she been awake? Doc did not respond and suddenly the little body just slipped out into the world and, after suctioning, began to whine. He handed me the baby to take to the nursery to do the things I had been trained to do. Through extra caution and plain old fear, it took me forever to get the baby ready for viewing. I decided I may want to be a pediatric nurse.

While passing the emergency room door one night, the alarm sounded, the doors swung open and the EMT's pushed a gurney into the exam room. Dr. Hart asked for my assistance in ER.

An elderly gentleman lay propped on his side as he moaned loudly. Dr. Hart requested a sterile scalpel pack. I prepared the pack and stood by to assist. The patient presented with a huge red pone protruding from the back of his head. After a few injections in various places surrounding the red area, the doctor picked up the scalpel and carefully lanced the knot.

Following the initial eruption from the incision, he picked up his tweezers. He probed in the hole for a few seconds and then began pulling out a white ropy substance. My stomach rebelled. I thought doc was pulling out brain matter. I guess Dr. Hart became aware of my situation when he heard my first pronounced gag. I had learned to not project my thoughts in front of patients, but I knew that if I did not retreat quickly, I would be projecting otherwise.

Dr. Hart completed his task alone, called the family in and sent the patient home. Then he found me still pale and lifeless in the dining room. He inquired as to why this simple procedure had bothered me so intensely. I really didn't want to tell him but I did. I told him that when he began pulling out that white stuff, I thought it was the man's brains. Dr. Hart was a very tall, dark and handsome man. He was always courteous, profession and caring with everyone. I sat amazed while he laughed so hard that he could not speak for minutes. He did apologize for laughing at me but it didn't help my feelings one bit. He explained that the white matter was the core to a carbuncle which is a major infected boil. I discovered a few days later that I was pregnant with my second child.

At the age of nineteen, I gave birth again. I quit working to stay home and care for our babies, but money was tight so while Rodney was still in diapers, I began searching for jobs. Over the next few years, I lasted one half day at a tomato canning factory, a few months at a cigar making factory, and finally found a great job at our local GE plant in Owensboro.

The ladies I rode with to work night shift at GE were worldly! I listened to their stories about sexual exploits, wild parties, and drinking times. I got drunk with them one night. Yep! As I sat at my machine making TV tubes, a small cup of clear liquid was passed to the girl next to me. She drank it and sputtered. Then the cup came back full and she handed it to me. I started to hand it to the next girl. No, she informed me that this one was mine. It was Christmas season. I gulped it down and didn't breathe forever. The cups continued through the night. Instead of my usual high production number, I constructed twenty tubes for the night, and I am not sure how many passed inspection. I have heard of bathtub gin. That is where I deposited the remains of my gin when I arrived home.

One very snowy night, we left our second shift job at GE. The snow covered streets were deserted. "Oh shit" Brenda yelled, as she eased to the deeper snow at the curb. "We are out of gas!"

In 1967, there were no cell phones. Before we could analyze our situation, a big Cadillac eased beside us. A black gentleman scooted across his front seat and opened the back door next to our stalled vehicle. I said nothing. Brenda asked us what we wanted to do. I honestly do not recall my answer, but Judy said we should just go to a house and knock on a door. Brenda opened her purse, took out a piece of metal, pushed a button, and a blade jumped out. Now I had something to say, but nothing came out. Brenda told us that she could protect us, so we climbed into the back seat of the rescuer's fancy car.

The man informed us that there was only one gas station in town that remained open all night. We instantly knew our driver was drinking. After slip-sliding across town, we arrived at the station. I still had not spoken.

The attendant came to the car and peered in to see three young, white, wide-eyed, ladies being escorted by an inebriated black man. I don't recall being upset that our rescuer was black; I just knew I did not want to wobble and weave those miles back across town. I expressed my desire to just walk home. Judy told me to just sit still and be quiet.

The lights from the gas pumps shone into the back floorboard of the car where my now nervous feet fidgeted. I noticed an object covered in a white cloth protruding from under the driver's seat. Curious, I placed my toe on the object and moved it into sight. There staring back at me was the blade of a huge knife wrapped in what looked like a bloody rag. My knees shook as I elbowed Judy who again told me to just be calm. Before I could get her attention, our rescuer suddenly opened my door. Lordy! Again, I remained speechless. I had moved what I thought was a murder weapon so that it was under my feet. The gentleman put his hand under the now empty space under the seat, said excuse me, and closed the door. He said he had dropped his cigarettes in the front floorboard and thought they may have slid under the seat. Now, my whole body shook. Brenda climbed in, and with cigarette in hand, steadied the full gas can which sat in the front seat.

When our Cadillac weaved to a stop beside Brenda's car, I bailed out of my door and ran so quickly that I'm sure I cleared a path for the others.

As soon as our car started, we left that poor man standing in the snow holding a gas can.

I arrived home just in time for my speech to return. I shook Tommy awake and screamed out my story. All he said was, "Why would you get in a car with a drunken man"?

The next day, I told my story to a neighbor who had lived in Owensboro all her life. She began laughing. She knew the man who had helped us. He was a well-known chef at a fancy restaurant in town. He was known for imbibing often. He also helped folks butcher animals after hours.

Tommy's construction job slowed; I was laid off one month after purchasing a new car and a new washer/dryer combo. We moved back to McLean County and after a while he landed a job at Tennessee Valley Authority. I went to work in a sewing factory.

The sewing factory was my introduction to unions, first hand. I wanted every penny I made to be put in my check to take home. The employer told me I had to pay dues and join a union for protection. I asked him from whom I needed protection. I discovered by working hard at piece work that I could make good money. The company soon hired me in administration as a trainer and floor supervisor. I then took all my pay home.

I enjoyed socializing and working with the folks at the factory. I listened to their concerns and tried to be patient as they struggled to learn their jobs. Then contract negotiation began. I had never been involved in a strike. I had listened to Tommy talk about scabs and other people who were not union. I never considered that I would be a target of hate because I wanted to work to help support my family. One Friday, while the company and union negotiated, I prepared to go home for the weekend. Some of the workers surrounded me outside my office. They scared the bejeebies out of me. One threatened to slash my tires if I reported to work when they had put up a picket line. One said to remember that I had a family! These were the same people I had called friends for years. I had been asked to work Saturday.

I actually shook all the way home. By the time I arrived in my driveway, my fear had turned to anger. Tommy informed me that I would not cross a picket line. Oops! Things were very unsettled in the Wilkerson household that night.

The next morning I received a call that the strike had been settled, and I would not need to report to work until Monday. That gave me two days to mull over and relate to the scene of Friday afternoon.

Monday, I was still shaking when I entered the building. After a company conference, I reported to my station. The only words exchanged among my workers and me were the orders I issued. I walked into the break room to a smiling, friendly group of folks who had ruined my whole weekend and family solitude. They had also shaken my faith in friendship. My little shoulder imp lead me through the next few moments. After a lengthy glare that silenced the room, I retired to a corner of my own. One girl asked me to sit by her. I told her to kiss my ass and to make sure she timed her break because I was timing all of them.

Shortly after that uncomfortable situation, I began a new career. I concluded that if one wants and needs the union, join. But, leave me to make my decision as to whether I want the same. I belonged to a union as teacher and even marched on the capitol at Frankfort,

Kentucky to keep the governor from raiding our pensions. I was not forced to participate.

Ardoth Hardin Wilkerson

CHAPTER 16

COLLEGE DAZE

You can get all A's and still flunk life.

--Unknown

A formidable structure facing Frederica Street in Owensboro, Kentucky, was just that to me until I made a decision which changed my life immensely.

Fifteen years into our marriage, we had managed to pay for a nice lot and mobile home overlooking Tommy's hometown of Island, Kentucky, population approximately 430. His job at Tennessee Valley Authority paid well, and I supplemented our income by working at a local sewing factory.

I had put an abrupt end to the five-child family by requiring a hysterectomy at the age of twenty-eight. Our two healthy, handsome boys, Tom and Rod, were then fifteen and twelve. Our finances were under control. We worked all week and then enjoyed our weekends camping, fishing, socializing or partying.

However, there remained in me the old desires to be a doctor, a nurse, teacher, or own a restaurant.

I announced to my husband that I would be attending college to become a teacher and girls' basketball coach. He waited a few days for what he considered my hair-brained idea to dissolve. Didn't happen! He reminded me that we would be paying for two college educations soon. Tom and Rod knew that their education included at least four years of college. They never entertained the idea of going into the work force without having choices. These were important goals for them from parents who had cut their education short to begin a family.

Having received a high school equivalency diploma a few years earlier, all I needed to start my new quest was to choose my college, find enough money to attend, and work hard. When I shared my news with a friend, she laughed and asked if I realized I would be in my thirties before I could complete a degree. I reminded her that I would be in my thirties anyway, so I might as well have a college education.

I climbed out of our new 1976 Ford Country Squire Station Wagon, which we had financed with money we had saved for a new home. My knees literally vibrated as I ascended the steps to enter that stately structure, Kentucky Wesleyan College. I had no idea which office door to enter. I carried a list of questions for someone, and knew that I would not leave until I was on my way back to a classroom. I was directed to the registrar's office.

I had withdrawn from LHS at the age of fifteen as a midterm sophomore, which meant that I was planning to enter a bachelor's degree program after having completed only nine years and four months of formal education. My previous fifteen years had been spent, birthing two sons, working at various public jobs, and keeping the home fires burning.

Gus Paris invited me into his office. I shared my dream. Mr. Paris mainly listened without reaction. Finally, I allowed him to speak. He spoke quickly using unfamiliar words and phrases. My resolve waned. Then, that little shoulder devil/Angel which has gotten me into and out of trouble many times vied for my attention. The words that came from me were not Angelic, but they were supposed to put me in a survival mode.

"Mr. Paris," I challenged, "I don't understand many of the words you are using. What is SAT? What is ACT? Lordy, what do you mean by matriculation fee? Do you have any money I may apply for?"

Silence!

When he finally spoke, it was with the same doubtful tone I had heard many times in the last few months. I listened and took notes. I left his office gripping an arm full of literature and on probation! Yes, because I had not taken the SAT or the ACT and my grade transcript presented only nine years of education, I would be on probation for the first semester. I could register for only nine credits and must make at least an average GPA.

Tommy, by this time had not only accepted my dream, he had begun rooting for me. He feared that the registration day may end my new goal. He smiled at my excited chatter all the way home.

The day to sign up for classes arrived! I squeezed and jostled my way among the hundreds of young in the Quonset hut as we chose our professors, classes, and time slots. I signed for a three hour course in English with Mr. Joe Britton. Then, probably knowing more history from firsthand experience than most of the students, I chose a basic history class. I had always wanted to speak a foreign language, plus it would be a part of my degree, so I enrolled in a German class with Dr. Weis.

I did not choose my clothes, for my first day of college, to make an impression. I chose what was laundered and comfortable.

Turning from Frederica Street onto campus, I mustered all my resolve to keep from driving straight through to stadium drive and heading back to familiar surroundings.

Neat, well-dressed, handsome, short stature, Mr. Britton walked into my first college English class. I knew I had made a good decision as soon as he began his welcome words. Now comfortable, sitting among mostly teens, which had already made me welcome, Mr. Britton made it official; I belonged. Our first assignment was a personal narrative.

After class, I sat in the main foyer contemplating the assignment. First, I needed to know exactly what a personal narrative entailed. Then I needed to stop somewhere to purchase a typewriter. Next, I needed to learn to type in three days.

Casual dress, tall, large build, Dr. Lee Dew authoritatively swaggered into my first college history class. He walked to the end of a large wooden desk and shoved it across the floor. The corner of the desk caught on the rug which ripped.

Silence reigned!

I looked around at the wide-eyed youths. He jammed his thumbs into his back pockets, paced the isle between the desks and welcomed us with his rules and his expectations.

Oops! I wondered, *do I belong here?* I wondered how long I could restrain my little devil that had already begun his tap dance on my shoulder. The assignment: reading and a work study sheet.

Dr. Weis stood at his desk as I entered my first foreign language class. I was the first student and only a few more arrived. He welcomed us and I settled in as I had in my earlier English class. After reading a few German words and demonstrating the guttural pronunciation techniques, we were given the task of learning a few phrases and verbs before our next meeting.

Still working part-time, taking care of my three men, a dog and a parakeet, I found myself studying into the wee hours of the morning. That first week set a pattern which I followed for the next five years. I tackled my English assignment first. While writing my narrative, the portable, blue Underwood typewriter taunted me from the back corner of the kitchen table. Before placing it there, I had only learned to open it and type a few short words. With pen in hand, my words flew easily across the pages as I wrote about giving birth to my first son sixteen years earlier. I wanted so badly to just neatly print my assignment and submit it. But, one of the main requirements was that it must be typed. Hours later I completed my first college assignment. At least, I thought so.

I easily completed the history assignment and

saved the German task for last. My throat didn't want to issue the same sounds that Dr. Weis had shared with us. While working through a few phrases and sentences, I came upon one that cracked me up. I practiced it using every possible pronunciation I had learned from two hours of language instruction. The English sentence read something like, "We traveled over Germany."

The German translation read, "Wir fahrt uber Deutschland."

Tired, but pleased, I pointed the wagon toward Owensboro, stopped at McDonald's near campus for a sausage sandwich, (another five year habit) and headed to a day of English, history, and German.

I submitted my writing to Mr. Britton, kept my ears perked and pen running as he lectured.

I dreaded Dr. Dew's history class. Again, I waited in the foyer, perused my history work sheets and practiced my German words.

No one had arrived in the history room, so I found myself a seat in the back avoiding the isle in case he wanted to pace again. I didn't want that little imp on my shoulder to cause my foot to jump out into the isle. Students trickled in and a few began talking about our first session. I listened! Most of them just laughed at his earlier macho behavior.

He arrived! His demeanor had not changed, but the students' attitudes toward him had. A few had dropped the class, but a few had joined. We listened intently, and I actually enjoyed hearing him share his vast knowledge of history. I even joined some of Dr. Dew's other history classes before I graduated.

German had fewer students than my other classes.

We took turns sounding words and reading phrases and sentences. "Mrs. Wilkerson, please read the next sentence in German," he requested.

My heart rate rose. The sentence he asked me to read was the one I had not mastered. In an almost inaudible voice, I read, "Wir farht uber Deutschland." When I read the word "farht" it came out so quickly that it had no distinct sound. He politely asked me to speak up and try to use better pronunciation. I felt the stares and sensed the fear in the other students that they may be called on to read the same sentence. I tried again. I tried a third time.

With hope-filled eyes I looked up at Dr. Weis. He smiled and loudly stated, "Now that would be stinky wouldn't it, Mrs. Wilkerson."

The class erupted in laughter. I think I saw sparks flying from my red face. We all relaxed and became better acquainted with a man who was not only very intelligent, but witty and full of humor. I actually earned many credits in German through the next five years, thanks to Dr. Weis.

My third day of college really changed my life. After my morning sausage fix, I reported to English class. Most of the time, I arrived early. That day Mr. Britton was setting up an overhead. In a few moments, I glanced up to see my paper plastered on the big screen. I knew I should run for home, but my feet wouldn't move. I thought the writing, I considered a labor of love, had turned into a spectacle that would send me home defeated. Other students appeared, each staring at my paper, which by this time seemed to me to be written in bright neon and pulsating on the screen. Although my name was not on the paper, the other students had to realize it was my paper because of the subject matter. Mr. Britton checked roll. He informed us that he had graded our first writings. I thought, *Just about the time I had decided I could do this college thing, something like this has to happen.*

Mr. Britton's first words were praise for most of our writings. Then he said that he wanted to share one that was so impressive he had set up the overhead to share it. I waited for him to choose one from his desk, instead; he pointed to my paper. He shared the contents of my paper, pointed out the descriptive straight forward words I had used and continued with his words of praise and encouragement. Unbeknownst to him, he had just created an English teacher. He took a red pen and placed an "A" on my paper. Those sweet young folks actually applauded. Then he turned to me and said, "Mrs. Wilkerson, learn to type." I did!

I learned to learn in college. My pea brain couldn't possibly carry all the information presented to me in those five years. One promise I made to myself was to ask questions if I didn't understand. I exercised my arm in many classes during those years. I figured that if I were paying for knowledge, I should get all I could. The younger students also appreciated the fact that I felt no shame in admitting my ignorance.

Not a single professor seemed to resent my requests until many years later I enrolled in my Master's program By that time I had been teaching for a few years and had established a good relationship with most of my students by respecting them and asking for their respect.

An English professor from Western Kentucky

University wrote a long, unfamiliar word on the board. I raised my hand and asked the meaning of the word. After a long pause, he asked me how I could be in a Master's program and not know the definition to his word.

Silence!

The other folks in the class were not all young. Many were older than I and a few younger. That little devil on my shoulder began doing the Kentucky clog dance. Red faced from anger, not embarrassment, I turned to my fellow students and asked anyone to define the word for me. Absolutely, no one knew the meaning of the word. Now it was Mr. Professor's time to turn red and angry. He never explained the word. He just continued his boring, self-indulging lecture. By the end of the class period, we knew where he spent his summers--Hampton's, I think, and we still needed to look up the word he had written on the board to try to impress us.

I had contracted for a "B" in his class because I wanted to complete my master's in one year while teaching full time. As long as I maintained a 3.0 GPA, all that mattered was that I could graduate soon and receive a large pay raise. I struggled through his class; we finally settled our clashes when I informed him that I knew the procedures for filing complaints and that I would pursue them to the fullest, starting with his pompous-ass attitude.

My senior year, I attended college with my son, Tom Jr., who was a freshman. He lived in a dorm on campus. Many times I would go to the dorm to visit him and each time one of the students would announce loudly, "Tom's Mom is here"! It took me a while to realize that the announcement was a warning not a greeting.

A few years later, I graduated from my Master's program the day after our youngest son received his bachelor's degree. Rodney received his degree with a major in biology, minor in chemistry, and associates in chemical engineering. Tom Jr. became a wonderful, caring registered nurse.

CHAPTER 17

TEACHING DAZE

I never teach my pupils; I only attempt to provide the conditions in which they can learn.

--Albert Einstein

My dear husband questioned me as to why I seemed tired after a day of teaching. As a pipe fitter/welder his work day consisted of constant physical exertion. Thus, I understood his question.

My answer to him, "When an educator, worth her salt, enters a place of learning which is flowing with students, there is mental radar which kicks in and remains alert until leaving the environment. I am constantly aware of where the students are, how they are relating to each other, and in the meantime, I am trying to reach them academically."

Yes, every teacher could, and many should, write a book. The interactions with my students contributed a major part of my enjoyment of teaching teens. While pushing my way through the maze of students in the hallways of McLean County High School, I was always aware of the potential for a sudden awaking of the hazardous hormonal interactions among the natives. Sometimes the awakenings brought forth a jealous tirade between two males or two females. Sometimes I had to put on a "cease immediately" face for two students who were so tightly embraced they cast one shadow.

My Ardoth radar kicked in one day during an afternoon break in our commons area. I left the faculty ladies' room after a quick visit. Hurrying toward the office to collect my mail, I passed many of my next period students, most of which were male. A buzz rippled across the commons so I immediately knew that something was amiss and exciting. In the short distance between the restroom and the office, I had picked up an audience of students. As I walked to the mail room, Marlene, an office worker came rushing my way. I had no clue! She quickly began pawing at my dress! I still had no clue! By this time, the whole viewing audience was worked into frenzy. You must remember I was covering only a short time span of seconds, not minutes. Finally, I glanced to my backside where Marlene was still flailing away at my dress. There exposed, and I do mean exposed, beginning at the waist area, was my right buttock and leg. I then had a clue. My dress and slip were tucked into the waistband of my panty hose.

Don't try to guess my emotions, won't happen! With Marlene's assistance, we manipulated and smoothed the underskirt and dress to cover my hams. I continued into the more private mailroom while the students scattered about to share their absolutely joyful experience of viewing a teacher's hind. I just stood motionless for a time. I looked at the door leading to the huge open student area. I listened to the noisy twitter generated by my "accident." Facing what I couldn't change, I walked through the crowd, which silently parted for me as if I were royalty. No one bowed though. Instead, they watched me as if expecting me to deliver a barrage of teacher orders to disperse or get to classes.

Embarrassing situations happen when there are hundreds of adults and teens interacting in the same environment five days a week. Toilet paper clinging to a shoe, upchucking lunch, pants unzipped, unexpected or purposeful flatulence, but this was different, oh, so different.

I didn't have time to draw upon the many clichés that have helped me survive some of my previous uncomfortable events. By the time I had reached my desk, checked my dress for the tenth time, and sat down, the bell rang.

Our school was built in the open classroom concept. There were four classes in session in one large room. Each class was separated from its neighbor by movable, six-foot dividers.

I waited and I waited!

I later learned that my students hesitated to appear from the other side of the divider because they did not know my state of mind, and they had no idea what to say or how to keep from laughing and hurting my feelings. They finally slinked in single file, heads bowed, not glancing my way. Instead of their usual greetings of, "How ya doin' Mrs. Wilk?" or "Hey,

Mamaw, what we doin' today?" they remained silent.

The commotion from the other three classes echoed through the thin walls as the folks shared their unique experience with their teachers and fellow students. Silence reigned supreme in my little room. We all just sat and stared at each other. I smiled an oops-smile. They smiled. Boog Humphrey, my sweet Boog, who has since died in a car accident, walked over to my desk, sat his skinny frame on the corner, swung his dangling feet a few times and announced loudly, "Mrs. Wilkerson, it didn't look too bad for an old teacher's butt."

I think we all exhaled at the same time. Our next breath brought forth laughter, smiling, and talking at the same time. My sweethearts gathered around my desk and for the first half of our instructional time, we discussed my mishap. I, of course, wanted to know how many had viewed my posterior. Many! Mostly males! They wanted to know how I felt after realizing what was happening. One gorgeous young lady said, "Mrs. Wilkerson, if that had happened to me, I would never come out into public again!"

A wide-eyed, clearly enamored young man responded, "If it ever happens to you, I will purpose marriage immediately."

We became one little cadre of people learning together that, this too shall pass, laughter can be a better healer than tears, life goes on, and we must choose how to live it.

Each sweetie hugged me before he left the room that day. Boog said, "I'll see you tomorrow Mamaw; I just hope I don't see as much of you."

I talked to myself the complete twenty minutes it

took me to drive the twelve miles to Island.

Needing gas, I pulled into Red and Lemon's station. Red was the witty one who always teased my boys when they were very young about eating dead chickens. I eased to the nearest pump and rolled down my window to ask for a fill-up. Instead of picking up the pump hose, Red casually leaned on the window frame. He wanted to know how my day had gone. He didn't just ask, he asked with a wide smile on his twinkling face. He could not know, I wondered. He did know. He knew enough to ask me why I had mooned the whole commons area. Lordy, I thought, *maybe this will not pass*. I expressed my desire that I just wanted him to fill my gas tank, remove the smile from his face, and ask no more questions. I don't blame him for his amusement at my new happening, after all, this was the same man who pointed out early one morning as he filled my gas tank, that I had a pair of red silk panties on my curled hair. He was also the fire chief who had to help push Island's old fire engine up a hill to extinguish my burning toilet I had set afire.

I then pondered as to how my two boys would react to the news. Any parent who has taught school knows that there is a rule that we never embarrass our own children. Amazingly, their reactions were to comfort me and laugh too.

Time to tell Tommy! His first words were, "Why did you do that?" I cannot relay to you the scene that followed or repeat the words that flew through our kitchen. He finally settled in with the fact that we could do nothing except live with it, whatever that meant.

The next school day, teachers came by to express their concern and sympathy. One would have thought I had lost a family member instead of my modesty. A well-intended, sympathetic teacher couldn't understand why I had not felt a breeze when I emerged from the restroom. Almost ten years later, she had a similar happening when her dress and slip adhered to a part of her anatomy. Her audience was smaller, just band members and a male teacher who swore he tried to punch out his eyes.

My students informed me that I had made news at some sporting events in other counties. On Valentine's Day, for years, people paid to have the chorus sing appropriate songs to me. Over our intercom, I listened to "Moon over Miami," or "Blue Moon of Kentucky." In the years that followed, the incident became a part of my self-introduction to incoming students. I always ended with the words, "Yes, I am the teacher who mooned the students in the commons area."

The youth I taught were so in tune to life. They amazed me with their knowledge of what I considered mature subjects reserved for the adult world.

Faculty and students at MCHS were fortunate to have a secretary who served as a lifeline to information, a hug buddy, and a friend to students and faculty. Willena's husband, Dean, worked as our janitor. They devoted their work days to their jobs but also contributed immensely to help keep our days running smoothly.

Willena, thinking I was working alone during my plan period, called over my intercom, "Ardie, Dean picked up your hormone meds for you."

I was not alone! The room was populated with

approximately thirty senior students. I smiled another of my oops- smiles.

Mr. Shocklee, a quick witted, comfortable, young man, sitting directly in front of my desk, proclaimed loudly, "Thank goodness." This gentleman is now a successful lawyer.

One of my first "oops moments" happened as I prepared to administer a test to a freshman class. A test taking technique I used was to stand in the back of a room so that I could observe test takers, but they could not observe me. After distributing papers and reminding them of the test procedures, I took my place in the rear area. A few folks glanced back to see where I was standing.

"I want all faces toward the front," is what I meant to say.

Instead I announced loudly, "All asses toward the front."

To this day, I have no idea how that word "faces" became "asses."

Of course, all faces turned toward me and watched my face turn red and smile my smile.

I suppose I left a mixed legacy in our school system. I enjoy hearing from my former students. I especially love to hear any positives I have performed in their lives.

Another day at MCHS delivered Tres to my freshman English class. His large football frame seemed to dominate the entry way as he ambled into the room to begin his first semester with a new teacher in a new environment. As most teachers know, ninth graders are an eclectic crew. They carry with them the middle school mentality, which they try to hide, as they try to carve out a place for themselves in the high school hierarchy. Tres had no intentions of waiting to be selected as a keeper by the upperclassmen. He was comfortable in his own skin and made that known to others and to me immediately.

Attempting to make the greenies comfortable in the big school on the hill, we spent most of our first meeting getting acquainted. I introduced myself, told them my expectations for them and asked what they expected from me as their teacher. By the end of our discussion we mostly agreed to treat each other as we wanted to be treated and decided to work together to enjoy together.

Reading and writing were and are two great pleasures in my life. Desiring to pass that passion on to my students, we read often and wrote constantly. I introduced one of my favorite readings, *Where the Red Fern Grows*. As I distributed the small novel, I shared a little background of the author and told just enough about the book to hopefully grab their interest.

Tres raised his hand. "Mrs. Wilkerson, I have never read a book in my life and really don't plan to start now," he challenged. He glanced around to survey for a doting audience. Uncomfortable giggles rippled across the room.

I continued my task as all ears waited for the answer to my first challenge. "Well, Mr. Settles, you have made working with this class so much easier. Thank You."

He turned his freckled face toward me. "And what does that mean?" he queried.

"Tres, it takes me a few seconds to record a zero

for your literature grades. The time I save with you, I can use in teaching those who want to learn and maybe participate in sophomore English next year."

I read the first few pages aloud. They continued reading until the end of class time. I then reminded them to deposit the books back on the table so I could use them in other classes.

Tres' father worked in our downtown central office. He was walking down the hall the next morning as I headed to my room. He wanted to know what I had done to his son the previous day. During the night he had arisen for a drink of water and noticed the light on in Tres' room. Tres was reading. I smiled.

I watched as Tres replaced his sneaked copy of *Where the Red Fern Grows* back onto the stack on the table.

Tres played football at our prestigious University of Kentucky, where he majored in English. He became a prolific reader, an English teacher, a vice-principal, a principal and is now serving as superintendent of our McLean County School System. If I were still teaching, he would be my boss!

My heart overflowed when I succeeded in reaching students through my love for them and my love for learning. But, I know that I just provided the nudge; they did the rest.

Ardoth Hardin Wilkerson

CHAPTER 18

ANNIE OAKLEY OF GREEN RIVER

Do you not know that I am woman? When I think, I speak.

--William Shakespeare

As retirement time grew near, we began clearing the nest and staying in our trailer on Green River. Our love of the shorelines continues today as we live at Whisper Creek near the Caloosahatchee River. But most of my foot and butt prints were made on the creeks and rivers in Kentucky. We stocked a few chickens and ducks. I so enjoyed quacking for the ducks and watching them paddle their cute webbed waders through the water. Folks in our area brought their families to see the pretty ducks.

As I walked out the camper door one day, I heard a loud, very close gunshot below our home. I immediately hurried to the river bank in time to see a man lower his gun. He had killed one of my tame ducks. Most of our ducks were white with orange bills, but we had a few that were black, red billed, hissing ducks which had no resemblance to wild ones. Tommy yelled at them, and they quickly turned to head down river. They had a small boat loaded with men and one child. We jumped into our boat in pursuit. Still wearing my pj's and housedress, I climbed to the front deck, screaming for this slow moving boat carrying men with loaded guns, to pull over. They, of course, did not.

We returned to our trailer and called the game warden. When the idiots docked in Calhoun down river, it happened to be the same time that most of the local law and wardens were taking a break at the restaurant next to the landing. They emerged from the boat confessing that they had killed a ladies pet duck and they would pay for it. The law gave us a choice of either naming a price for the duck or allowing the law to take them to federal court. We chose the court. The men testified that the young boy had done the shooting. The youth received a reprimand and the duck hunters were banned from Green River. What terrible role models for that young man?

Another incident involved two drunks trying to catch the ducks by their necks. We were awaked by the sound of a motor boat revving loudly. We ran to the deck in time to see two males in a boat which was running in a tight circle. It flipped over spilling the passengers, coolers, fishing gear, and tanks into the river. I applauded. As one clung to a cooler and another held onto the side of the overturned boat,

Tommy dressed quickly. Large coal tugs ran constantly. I asked him to leave them on their own. Lordy, now you know the real me. I despise people who want to hurt animals, especially the ones I feed.

By the time Tommy had reached our boat, we could hear the sound of a barge coming up river. The male on the cooler had kicked his way to the shore, while the one gripping the boat remained in the middle of the river. Tommy pulled him to safety and helped him upright the boat. He warned them that he would be watching for them and they would not have to wait for a boat to overturn to be in danger. He left them as they tried unsuccessfully to start their motor. The last time we saw them they were using a gas can to paddle out of our area.

A quiet afternoon, I sat on our deck reading. I usually just glanced at the recreation boats as they passed our home. A large speed boat loaded with Sunday partiers made a quick U-turn and headed for the area near my deck where I sat. Before my mind could even comprehend what the driver had planned, he sped directly through the flock of unsuspecting ducks. Anger takes away logic. I hurried to the bedroom and picked up Tommy's big hand gun. Returning to the porch, I aimed directly at the boat and cocked the hammer. The boat driver circled and started his assault again. Just before I pulled the trigger, a girl spotted me and screamed, "She's got a gun!"

The driver aborted his mission and raced down river. Tommy heard the commotion. He came around the corner just as I lowered the gun. Scared that man to pieces! I knew they would have to come back my way to a ramp up river. Tommy confiscated the gun, but I waited. Just before dark, I heard a boat in a hurry. It remained as close as was safe to the far shore and sped by without a passenger in sight. I could barely see the driver's hand as he steered away from that old gun- toting grandma. Tommy decided that it would be wise to give my ducks to a farmer friend.

CHAPTER 19

TOM AND ROD AND ACCIDENTS

All the world is full of suffering. It is also full of overcoming.

--Helen Keller

In 1977, we decided to take a trip to the west before another school and college semester began. Tommy and I had survived to reach the ages of thirty-five and thirty-two respectively. Rod was twelve, and Tom Jr. at sixteen had just received his driver's license. What sixteen-year-old wants to go anywhere with his parents and another old couple, especially for a week and especially miss his first day of school driving his own Ford Maverick.

After much debate, begging, rules, and promises, we relented and agreed to allow Tom Jr. to stay with Aunt Zeula. That worked very well because Tom Jr. actually had no one his age traveling with us. He was a high school junior involved in football and other school activities.

The second night in Colorado, we called to check on Tom Jr. He informed us that he and his buddy Stevie had hit a ditch, but it was in Stevie's car and everyone was fine. Mom radar kicked in. I called Aunt Zeula. She told me that he was coming home on time and all was well.

A week later we headed for home. Our second day on the road was also the opening day for McLean County Schools. I knew what a proud moment that was for all the new drivers to pull into the parking lot and circle a few times so the other students could check the ride and driver.

We stopped at a new Wendy's restaurant in Henderson, Kentucky. I went in to order and noticed a gentleman and his wife from Island were having lunch. I spoke to them. He asked me how our son was doing. I wanted to know which one he was asking about. Then he asked me if he was in the hospital in Evansville. I could not understand his question. After a glance at his wife, he asked me if we had been out of town. I told him that we were just returning from a trip. He then asked where Tommy was. Then I remembered the ditch incident. I told him that Tom Jr. and Stevie had hit a ditch a few days ago, but they were fine. He told me to get Tommy because he needed to tell me something. I hurried to the car.

Tom Jr. and Stevie had been involved in a serious accident on the way to school that morning and there had been no way to contact us. They were both in the Owensboro hospital.

I cried the whole forty mile trip to Owensboro. The pictures in my mind frightened me so that by the time we arrived at the hospital, I was shaking from head to toe. Later, family members who lined the hallway, said they could hear me before I even left the elevator.

I did not recognize Stevie. I barely recognized Tom Jr. Blood and glass were still on them and on the beds. They were zonked on pain medicine but both still crying.

As a mother who had sheltered his tiny body under my heart for nine months and then tried to shelter him for sixteen years, I felt I had finally failed. Dr. McKay appeared. He sent a nurse to bring two valiums which he handed to me and ordered me to take immediately.

Stevie suffered from a broken nose, femur, and serious cuts and contusions over his body. Tom Jr. had fifty stitches in his head where the scalp had been torn from his skull. He had a broken wrist, ankle, femur and numerous cuts and contusions.

I spent the next month traveling from home to classes and the hospital to be with Tom Jr. I helped bathe him, took them treats, and did my homework while they slept. The girls from their school loved to go to the hospital to sit on the edge of their beds. They loved it when the girls sat on the edge of their beds.

One day as I entered their room, a new nurse was attending to Tom Jr. She asked me to step out until she had finished helping him bathe. I did. When I returned Stevie was clearly amused about something. Tom did not seem to share his glee. The new nurse had asked me to step out because she thought I was Tom's girlfriend. My grin was ear to ear.

He suffered so much, and I suffered the blame game. If only I had made him go with us. If only I had not given him my car. The boys spent twenty-nine days in the hospital. Then Tom Jr. had to return for a second surgery because a bone particle had broken loose in his leg, and the metal rod placed in his leg was too long and had to be removed.

Recover is another word with a broad definition. I don't think Tom ever fully recovered from his head trauma. He still suffers from headaches in the same area of his injury. He still walks with a slight limp. When he attends to trauma patients, his memory many times returns to 1977.

I will never recover completely. The fear remains and as Tom Jr. returned to driving, Rod started driving, and each grandchild receives a license, I remember.

ROD'S ACCIDENT

The following pages are the papers submitted to the lawyers.

May 5th, 2006, Rodney entered a hospital to have gallbladder surgery. Approximately twenty minutes after taking him to surgery, his surgeon, asked to see us in a conference room. Pam, Tom Sr. and I, went in. He told us that they could not intubate him and that he could not perform the surgery that day. He said that even if they were to succeed in the intubation, that he had too much air in him to operate that day. He was noticeably nervous, and he stated that this had never happened to him before. He mentioned nothing about a problem with losing a piece of equipment in Rod. We questioned him as to Rod's surgical status, and he told us that he would discuss that with us in his office on Tuesday, May 9th. He also said that his gallbladder was not a life threatening situation. He said they would allow him to awaken and send him home.

Shortly after our conference with the doctor, Pam went in to see Rodney. She came back tearful and informed us that the anesthesiologist had lost a piece of medical equipment inside Rodney. They were not sure where it was, but they needed permission to go in and find it. We then met with another doctor from gastroenterology. He said if it were in Rod's stomach, they would keep him for a while to see that it passed. Pam questioned him as to the possibility of an obstruction if they waited for it to pass. He said that should not be a problem. Then we were taken to another part of the hospital where we met another doctor, an ENT. We were informed that the piece was in his esophagus. By this time our concern had turned to fear. I asked the ENT what the next step would be if he could not retrieve the piece. He stated very quickly and emphatically, 'I can get it out.'

We were then taken to the third floor same-day surgery waiting room. Over four hours later we were still waiting. Pam called for updates. They would say that they had pushed it into his stomach and still could not bring it up. My question at that point was that if the doctors had been so confident that he could pass it safely, then why did they continue to delve into his throat and pull it up then push it back down.

Finally, I became almost hysterical, so they sent two nurses from the OR to talk to us. I told them that if they could not do this surgery safely, that I wanted him sent somewhere else. They said they had never encountered *this type of problem before so they needed time to figure out how to retrieve the piece. We sat down again. A short time later, a doctor appeared to tell us that they had recovered the object. Rod was in surgery five hours.*

A doctor took us to another conference room to show us the type of object he had removed. He explained why it had taken so long to get it out of him. He also said that they would be contacting the vendor about the problem. He said that he wanted to keep Rodney on the vent for 48 hours because of possible swelling from the surgery. He also said he wanted him to be in the OR when it was removed. He stated that the 48 hours would be up Sunday but because of lack of staff, that he would wait until Monday to remove him from the vent.

Rod was moved to intensive care, kept on sedation and morphine. Pam stayed by his side until Sunday. She called to tell us that he had slight pneumonia in one lung on Sunday. Tom Sr. and I asked for help with the children so we could go to the hospital. When we arrived at the hospital, Pam asked me not to leave his side because she had been having to ask them to suction him and more than once they had almost let his sedation run out. She showed me the bags to watch closely.

While I was there Sunday, they came in and put pressure hose on his legs. The lady who put them on had to get someone else to show her how to put them on correctly. When they pumped up, it thoroughly bothered Rodney. When Rod would try to sit up in bed, I would try to comfort him. He seemed to be trying to gasp for breath and cough. I called for the nurses. Sometimes they came; sometimes they said that he was just trying to cough and that he would be fine. Once he rose up and turned red, then a blue purple color. I became very anxious and insisted that someone come in. A nurse came in and suctioned him. He calmed down again.

Monday, a doctor said that his pneumonia was the same. About 11 a.m., they came in to prepare him for removal of the vent. Tom Sr. and I went to the third floor same day surgery room. About an hour later, Pam came up and said that they would not be removing the vent because a doctor advised against it.

We later learned through personnel who worked in ICU that no one wanted to go into the OR to remove the tube. The ENT would not go in and the anesthesiologist would not do it alone. When we arrived back in ICU, Pam needed to go home to get clothes and attend to matters for the children. Rodney's oxygen level continued to drop. The nurse called the doctor. He/she said to add more Lasik and turn up his oxygen. He/she also ordered a chest x-ray to look for blood clots.

We talked about where to move Rod, because we were now more than just fearful. It was a feeling of dread like I have never known before. Pam said that she would call some folks at Red Cross where she works for advice. I asked the nurse when they were going to try to get him off the vent, and she said it would be days at least. I informed my husband who called our son who is an RN. He took off work and started to Elizabethtown. I then called our local doctor in Whitesville, KY, and asked his advice. I told him that we were very unhappy with Rod's care and wanted to move him. He told us the correct procedure to use to get him moved.

When our son arrived, he asked many questions that we did not know to ask. He found various problems with his care and stated that we were correct in trying to get him special help. I was not as involved in his transfer as Tom Jr., Pam, and Tom Sr., I just knew that the folks in ICU were whispering and conferring and some seemed concerned that the doctors were not helping us with the transfer. I watched as one of Rod's doctors came down the hallway. She started to walk by us, but Pam caught up with her. She continued to walk as Pam asked her about Rodney's blood clot. She said that it was just a tiny one, nothing to be concerned about. I didn't hear any more of that conversation. Tom Jr., Pam and Tom Sr. can relate the experiences they had with hospital personnel while trying to get help to transfer Rodney.

After three hours of trying to get Rod transferred, we were all very frustrated and probably seemed to some of the staff to be very aggressive people. My husband saw one of the ICU personnel leaving and patted her on the back and explained to her that we were not bad people; we were just concerned about Rodney's care. She told him that if it had been her loved one, she would have moved him much earlier. We think she was the unit clerk because she was doing most of the telephoning. She said that she became concerned when no one would go into the operating room to remove Rod from the vent. She said that the anesthesiologist would not do it alone. At this point no doctor wanted to be involved in this case.

My husband also told me that when a doctor heard about his transfer to Jewish, she told him that he was not an emergency. She also said that she had other patients to attend to and was very condescending until Tom Jr. began to speak and let her know that he is medically literate.

I don't want to sound as if I am the only one to have

ever experienced the possible loss of a child, but I know that anger and grief do not mix well. I tried to forget the anger and concentrate on praying for my son, but when the doctors at Jewish told us how very ill Rodney was, I couldn't forget the fact that it seemed so unnecessary for by son to be going through such an ordeal. As I thought of his four young sons and how they would be so devastated, I discovered that I am a weak person. My husband had had two heart attacks in the last nine months, but he was my rock. Tom Jr. knew more about Rod's medical condition than we, so his fear was even more profound than ours. I watched my son almost die. I worried about my husband's heart condition as he suffered with the possible loss of our son. I watched as Tom Jr. tried to be brave and tried to give us bits of good news, although Rod's condition was worsening. I watched Rodney's wife as she struggled with how to tell the boys that their Dad was very serious, but yet not alarm them. She used all her leave time, and because she carried their insurance, she had to go back to work so that she would have a paycheck.

I know that I will never be the same. In my 61 years on earth, I have suffered through many battles, but this one with Rod has left an open wound. I almost lost Tom Jr. in 1977 and 2004 and my husband in 2005. I will never heal. I know that. I have a new awareness inside me. I know now how it feels to be told that I may lose my family. I also know that I am not strong. I am praying every day for more strength and understanding.

I have never been a proponent of lawsuits, but someone should be held accountable for the horror my precious family has suffered.

The following pages are notes from Tom Jr.

Upon arrival, I discovered HOB flat, 02 sat at 87%, inverted T wave, CT had been done to check for PE, but report had not been checked. No orders had been given for anticoagulants or Doppler studies. Seg teds were in place. EKG had been normal (without inverted T wave) upon admission. When I questioned the nurse, she said she did not know when the rhythm had changed. Nurse was not going to address this until I requested an EKG. CE not done.

After encountering these problems with his quality of care, I told Pam that I felt she should proceed with her plan to transfer Rod to Jewish. Pam initiated this process, but was told that she would have to find Rod a doctor at Jewish. Pam began trying to reach people who could help find a doctor. When I learned of what the personnel had told Pam, I asked for the house supervisor. He appeared and after whispering around the nurses' station for a while, he came to see me. I told him that I wanted them to start making arrangements immediately for Rodney's transfer, because it was not Pam's responsibility that her responsibility was to be by her husband's bedside. He stated that he would get started with the process.

A pulmonologist was in charge of Rod's care, however, his wife, a hematologist, came to see Rodney that evening. She listened to his lungs for about ten seconds and then asked why we thought he needed to be transferred. In a very flippant manner she said, 'After all, he is not having a heart attack or needing open heart surgery or bleeding out.' She said he was not an emergency. I asked her what her plan was for his care and she stated that she would start him on Heparin and continue to monitor his condition. I then stated that Rodney had come in for a simple lap choly and now he was on life support and in acute respiratory failure with his condition deteriorating by the minute. I asked her why she felt that his situation did not fall under emergency guidelines. My father asked her if she would be available if needed and her curt answer was that she could not stay around there because she had other patients. I became very upset and told her not to be condescending with us that my brother was lying in front of us possibly dying and not being given the proper care. She told me to calm down because there was no reason to be upset. I told her that we have a very valid reason to be upset and that I wanted her to proceed with Rodney's transfer. She then said, 'Well, I will have to stop talking to you to do that.'

She left the room. After writing orders and making phone calls, she never came back to wish us well or even inform us as to his transfer status. I watched as one of the staff members began making fun of our situation. She grabbed the around the neck in an aggressive manner and pretended to shake her while looking toward Rod's room and both were laughing. Mom told me later of watching as two ICU personnel made fun of grieving family members who had lost a loved one in the ICU unit. I know that has nothing to do directly with Rod's care, but it does say something about the character of some of the folks who hold precious lives in their hands daily.

RODNEY UPDATED

Because of incidents during and after his surgery, Rodney was transferred to Jewish Hospital in Louisville. After a full-alert trip to Jewish, he was quickly admitted while five specialists stood by to attend to his dire medical condition. They evaluated Rodney's condition and informed us that they would do all in their power to save our son. If he lived seventy-two hours, there would be more hope. Here I go again with the lack of words to describe my feelings. First, I wanted to return to the other hospital and maybe just hurt some folks. What could that change? I then gave in to the fact that I could not "fix" this boo-boo for Rodney and that I must find strength through my faith in God. No, God did not take away my fears and anger. He simply listened and held my hand as I cried, screamed, cursed, pleaded, denied, and prayed. I promised Him everything except my second born son.

I did not see my son again for almost seventeen days. He was on life support and sedated. I was and am so weak: even though God is my strength, this earthly body and mind just gives in to grief. Tom Jr., Tom Sr., and Pam loved on him during the scheduled visits. I sat in the waiting area for those many days and anxiously awaited any news of my son. Because Tom Jr. is a nurse, Pam signed papers that allowed him to help make decisions and to be privilege to medical information concerning Rodney.

With the support of God, love for his brother, and Jewish doctors, Tom Jr. helped save his brother's life. As I reflect on those sad days, I can only imagine the pain Tom Jr. lived through while trying to deliver hopeful news to his family as he watched his brother possibly dying.

The day they removed the life support, Tom Jr. was allowed to be present. The family waited, praying he could breathe on his own. If not, he would be in for other serious medical procedures. Tom Jr. entered the waiting room with the thumbs up sign. I entered the ICU room to see my son. He had just been told that he had lost almost three weeks in his life. He lay crying and trembling trying to absorb the news.

We never heard from anyone involved in Rodney's care at the other hospital. At that point in our horrible journey, all we wanted was assurance that the incident would be addressed in some why that would maybe prevent this happening to someone else.

The doctors could not assure us that he would ever fully recover physically or mentally. He still struggles with long and short-term memory. His doctors said that because of his medical problems in 2006, he would always be susceptible to blood clots.

Rodney did not want to file a lawsuit. I insisted that we obtain counsel. The local attorneys informed us that it would be such a complicated case, involving so many institutions and people, that it would take years and too much money to file a lawsuit. I then wrote a letter to the other hospital's administrator, pleading for people to take responsibility for the incident. I wanted to speak to them face to face and let them see the anguish and pain that resulted from Rod's stay in their facility.

In March of 2009, Rodney had a knee replacement. He developed serious blood clots in both legs that have left him totally disabled. Before submitting this Rodney story, I again offered folks at the "other hospital" to address our situation. Didn't happen.

Howard Thomas Wilkerson Jr.

Rodney Lynn Wilkerson

CHAPTER 20

NOT GOOD AT GOODBYES!

We only part to meet again.

--John Gay

By the age of nineteen, I had lost two brothers and a school friend. I reflect often on the word "lost" when I experience that familiar empty ache in my heart. It is another word in our twenty-six letter alphabet that I use because I cannot find any other all-encompassing way to express my feelings. "Lost" infers that something is gone but may be found. That's fine with me because I sincerely believe that my loved ones are lost to me here on Earth, but I will find them again living in the arms of God. Those thoughts should carry me through my grief, but I am weak and I am selfish.

November 1st, 1965, Dad asked Tommy and me to take him to see a doctor. His told us his left arm ached and he had difficulty breathing. The only time I had ever seen him needing medical attention was when he had a broken arm and once when he suffered severe burns from a bed fire.

We took him to a local doctor, who sent him directly to the McLean County Hospital. Dad wanted us to take him home first to get some pajamas, so he said. He then wanted to go by Mom's home to see Mom, Yvonne, Janice and our two sons. As we left Livermore and turned toward Calhoun, for the second time in my life, I saw tears in my Dad's eyes. I honestly never once during that day's events thought that I may lose my Dad. We called my brothers and stayed at the hospital until closing time.

He died early the next morning on, Rodney, our youngest son's first birthday. Dad was fifty-nine. Being so young in my faith and so naïve about mortality, I suffered like a child without the ability to comprehend death. I suppose I went through the various stages of grief, but all I remember was thinking that I would no longer hear his whistling as he worked in my garden. I would no longer watch him stir gravy with his old crooked arm. He wouldn't be chugging into my driveway in his old pick- up truck. Dad's death left me angry.

In 1988, Gary, the brother I had tried so hard to know, the man who had weaved in and out of my adult world, loved but feared, died from a heat stroke. I wanted my brother to live as a normal person with a wife and children and the loving challenges that go with a marriage. Instead, he spent his fifty-nine years on Earth fighting the daily challenges of a diseased mind.

Eugene's granddaughter arrived November 9th,

1993. The family knew that Gena Rose Whittaker would be an Earth Angel for only a short time. Her sweet name was a combination of the names of Eugene and his wife Rosalie. The tiny casket that held Gena Rose also held the broken hearts of many. January 1994, as the cold, windy, sleet and snow covered our world, Gena Rose embraced the warmth of her Heavenly Father.

I smiled. Mom smiled. She reached toward me, and I tenderly rubbed warmth through her crooked, arthritic hands.

"Mom, you look better today; how do you feel?" I asked.

"I just want to go home," she replied.

Home? What home? I wondered if she meant the other nursing home, her neat little home by the river, her tiny apartment in my side yard or the spare bedroom in my house. She really didn't care where she went; she just knew that this plastic, vinyl world that she existed in now was not home. She wanted to fluff her old feather pillow. She wanted to roll over in bed without staring at chrome bars. She wanted to dress herself in her own threadbare cotton dresses and petticoats which were not labeled with black permanent marker. I wanted to make all these things happen for her, but I couldn't, not this time.

"Mom, do you want me to take you for a ride in your chair?" I asked. She managed a half-hearted nod.

We approached the main foyer where shafts of sunlight brightened the gray walls and floor. I desperately needed that reminder of my other world, and I resisted the urge to hurry toward the bright light. I wondered if that light could take me back to a time when Mom and I rose early to make biscuits for Dad and my seven brothers and sisters. I needed to experience again the time when I had been the Easter Sunday belle in my hand-sewn Easter dress Mom had made from a set of curtains. I didn't want my present life with my husband, children, and grandchildren to disappear. I just wanted to remember the good parts of my past and make things better now. I wanted to change Mom's inevitable future.

Finding a quiet corner room filled with plants and the odor of stale cigarette smoke, I shared the usual news of the weather, children, and grandchildren. She listened quietly. I really didn't want to just talk. I wanted to lie on Mom's lap and cry and tell her how sorry I was for all the times we had disagreed. I wanted to thank her for staying awake until 3: am to hand sew my Easter dress. I wanted to thank her for the ice cream she put in my Nehi orange drink when I had the measles. I wanted to thank her for teaching me to make biscuits. But, I knew that if I said those things, we would both have to admit that she was very old and very ill and that we were both very sorry for many things. We would have to deal with our fear for her tomorrows.

I just guided her wheelchair down the hallway toward her room. Turning a corner to enter the personal care wing of the nursing home, we suddenly heard a loud, squeaky voice singing, "Let me call you sweetheart, I'm in love with you."

Mom smiled. I smiled.

First I heard a low, almost inaudible hum. Then a definite, "Let me hear you whisper that you love me too," came from Mom as she made the solo a duet. A perky little aide attending our concert wanted to be anywhere except in that smelly hallway listening to two old ladies howling, "Daisy, Daisy." Relishing their enjoyment and remembering many of the old songs that Mom and Dad had sung to us, I joined in to form a trio. The little aide finally escaped, leaving a feisty old blind woman with one shoe missing, and my Mom and me to delight in our own renditions of, "She'll be coming around the mountain," and "The Old Mill Stream."

Thoughts of the past and of my late Dad brought back that dreadful empty ache that I had forgotten for the last few Moments as we shared our version of "Precious Memories." The trio became a solo as Mom began to sing "The Old Rugged Cross." Through touch more than sight, I managed to find Mom's room and quickly kissed her wet cheek. "See you in a few days; I love you," I said, as I hurried to the sunlight.

Mom died shortly after our nursing home trio debut. When I lose a loved one, I search my past for comfort and forgiveness for deeds undone and words unspoken. I am comfortable feeling that instead of leaving words unspoken between us, Mom and I, with the help of a little old blind lady, were able to share a healing harmony of words as we sang our last songs together.

Aunt Zeula passed from this life as Tom Jr. sat on one side of her bed and caressed her sweet, knotty, ninety-two-year-old hand. I gently held her other hand to watch her take her last earthly breath. The main role she played in our lives was the role of a mentor who taught by example. Both of our sons cherish, as many do, her memory. They speak of her often with love and praise.

When I lost Vonnie, in 2001, I lost my baby and my playmate. She loved life, she loved baby dolls, she loved family and friends, and God loved her. She seldom left our home, thus most people only knew her as a shadow in the Hardin family.

At her funeral viewing, most of the folks who came to visit did so to comfort the family and they actually saw her for the first time.

However, as a few older folks and a few family members sat in the Muster Funeral Parlor, the large back doors swung open. The staff and most of the residents from her nursing home entered. I had been fairly controlled until those precious challenged people entered the room. Some used canes, some sat in wheel chairs, some walked with others' assistance, but they all came to tell our baby girl goodbye. Vonnie's roommate placed a stuffed animal in the casket, touched her face, and cried.

Special times are for special people. Vonnie was special. I tried to let everyone who mattered know that we loved them and appreciated them. We placed these humble words in the local paper as Vonnie's goodbye.

Thank you friends for sharing your love with us during the loss of our sweet Yvonne (Vonnie). She loved hugs, laughter, good food, pretty flowers, flop-eared rabbits, baby dolls, Santa (Deller-Deller) and people. Every hug that you shared reminded us of her. The many memories you shared reminded us of her smiles and laughter. Brother Ron Hampton reminded us that she was truly unique. Brother Steve Murphy delivered a heartfelt eulogy that reminded us to cherish her simple innocence. You sent those pretty flowers that she loved. Tom Jr., Chris, Chad, Jason, Ryan, and Daniel gently carried her to a resting place beside her Mom, Dad, and brothers. Vonnie's Rosedale family came to tell her goodbye and to bring her gifts; they gave us a gift of precious memories that will forever comfort us. Brenda Chinn, Miller's Market, Donna Moore, Livermore Baptist Church, Mr. and Mrs. Carman, and Bonnie Hardin fed us. The Muster Funeral Home family compassionately led us through the emotional final arrangements. We send to all of you, from us, many Vonnie hugs.

    Love,
    Oliver and Sheila Hardin family,
    Eugene and Rosalie Hardin family,
    Tommy and Ardoth Wilkerson family,
    Steve and Janice Murphy family

Our baby sister, Jaybug, has been anything but a baby in her faith. While depending upon their strong faith, love of family and friends, she and her husband Steve buried two of their children in less than two years.

Jaybug called me to ask if Tom Jr. knew how she could get Chris, her oldest son, to a doctor who may be able to help his back problem. Before I could contact Tom Jr., she called back to tell us that Loretta, Chris' wife, had taken him to the emergency room. His legs had collapsed. Being a large man, he had had to drag himself to the vehicle and pull himself into the seat. They took him into the emergency room in a wheel chair. After an examination, his doctor decided he could go home on medication. Chris and Loretta asked how they were to manage since he could not use his legs. The doctor finally decided he would admit him and run a few more tests. The tests revealed terminal, advanced cancer in his spine. The emergency room doctor went to the family to apologize. I applaud him for that.

A few days later, Chris at the age of thirty-eight, was wheeled into the delivery room to welcome his ninth child into the world. Chris went to be with his savior at the age of thirty-nine.

The phone rang early at our son's home on May 6th, 2010. I answered. Jaybug calmly asked to speak to Tom Jr. I took the phone to his room, awakened him and started to walk away when I heard him say, "Oh, no Aunt Janice." Even in her unbelievable grief, she wanted someone to tell me in person that her sweet daughter, Tammy, had just died in a car accident. They said goodbye to Chris, July 27th, 2008. Less than two years later, they said goodbye to Tammy, on her thirty-ninth birthday, May 5th, 2010.

CHAPTER 21

WRITING DAZE

Be yourself. Above all, let who you are, what you are, what you believe, shine through every sentence you write, every piece you finish.

--John Jake

For years I have expressed my thoughts and feelings on paper. In 1986, I enjoyed a summer writing course as part of my Master's degree studies at Western Kentucky University. I learned to share my writings as a way to receive feedback from someone other than a family member. I submitted the following short story to our local newspaper, The Messenger/Inquirer. When the call came that my entry had been judged as first place, I asked if there had been more than two entries. I felt so proud when I learned that there had been many entries from seven counties. Some of my friends read this story to their children or grandchildren each Christmas.

Can Rudolph Swim?

Snowflakes fell lazily from a cheerless December sky and merged with the swift, murky Green River floodwater. A few of the white crystals hitched a ride on snow-covered driftwood that twisted and twirled its way toward a rendezvous at the mouth of Rough Creek.

Peering at the scene from her tiny loft bedroom, Sara Nell leaned her forehead against the cold, frosty window and cried. Sara had lived all her six years on the banks of that beautiful, sometimes sassy river. Her life was bluegills dancing at the end of her cane pole, twin fawns cautiously nibbling in the turnip patch, and hummingbirds darting among the red sage clusters.

Christmas mornings she snuggled in Grandma's old quilt by the open fireplace as her papa prodded the smoking, grey embers to life.

Rolling rushing waves that covered the turnip patch, the red sage beds and rest of Sara's Green River world, now threatened to seep into her cozy cabin home. Each day brought new fears and questions from little Sara Nell. "Mama, do you think Santa knows that I want a red coat with a rosebud collar for Christmas? Mama, if Santa misses our rooftop, can Rudolph swim?"

The mornings found Sara at her window anxiously watching the water creep toward the notch in the old beech tree near the well house. When the brown swirls covered that notch, they and many others along the river would have to move.

Christmas Eve night, before climbing into bed,

Sara did what she had done many cold winter nights. She moved her rag rug from the knothole in her floor and put her face near the small opening to feel the warm air against her cheek. She did not plan to be caught up in her parents' conversation, but when she heard her best friend's name mentioned, she pressed, one ear to the opening. Her mother was very concerned about Skeeter Wilson, a fragile little neighbor boy who lived about a mile upstream near Small House. Mama felt that the move in the damp weather could mean death for him if he became ill.

Sara covered her tiny porthole and knelt to pray. "Hello, God, I need your help. Please talk to Ole Miss Green River and tell her to go back home. Skeeter is my friend, and I don't want him to die. And God, I asked Santa for a new coat. If you could catch him before he leaves the North Pole, tell him to make that coat I asked for a little smaller and deliver it to Skeeter. Oh, also ask Santa to leave off the rose bud collar - Skeeter's a boy. I love you, God. Amen. Sorry, just one more thing; can Rudolph swim?"

Christmas morning Sara Nell scurried down the wooden ladder and watched as her papa stirred the resting fireplace embers to life. The flames cast a dancing, shadowy light into the corner where the holiday pine stood guard over a beautiful red coat with a rosebud collar. Hurrying to the nearest window, Sara erased the frost flowers with her open palm and squealed with delight. The rushing water that had been menacingly reaching for the tree notch was now slipping back to its own home. Christmas really was a time for joy after all.

Sharing Some of My Poetry

Now I Know!

As a child, I peered cautiously at the caterpillar
tip-toeing across the dusty road.
I wondered where he came from, where he was
going, if he would bite.

As a little lady, walking to school one day, I tried
not to look at the puppy lying deathly still on the side
of the busy road.
I wondered where he came from, where he was
going, and why he had to die.

As a teenager, I watched a new student enter our
classroom, and the teacher seated her beside me.
I wondered where she came from, how long she
would stay and why her skin was so dark next to
mine.

As a young mother, I stared at my baby's tiny
fingers, tiny toes, and sweet, sweet innocence.
I wondered where he really came from, what he
would eventually do in life, and if I deserved such a
miracle.

As a wife, mother, and grandmother who decided
to open my heart to God, now I know. I know that if I
do not have the answers, He does, and He will freely
share, if I ask.

This is for our band member and friend Tommy Taylor who passed on in 2010. Scoot and Violet host our music sessions. The band consists of folks from Florida, Indiana, Michigan, Canada, Kentucky and Wisconsin. We come together in November and most head north by April.

Rocking Chair Memories

The Scoot and Violet crew is like a puzzle with missing pieces when we all scatter about.

But we know where Everyone belongs, their needs, their cares.

Remembering how we all laugh and play together will make great memories for our old rocking chairs.

Our creator has granted us precious time to share lives and to love, to play, to care, to pray, to smile, to hurt, to cry, and many times to say goodbye.

When one of us receives God's call, we depend on each other to keep our little family strong.

But we'll all be together again, because God knows that is where we belong.

My Times

I have my times.
I must remember the paths.
One of my times wraps me in sweet nostalgia as I
sit on my old, wrought iron bench atop the wooden
bridge which spans our tiny farm lake.
It is my time to relax, remember or forget.
I enjoy the gorgeous sunsets that double their
beauty by reflecting in the blue waters beneath me.
Even when my grandchildren have gone home,
I still hear their laughter as they cast their bobber
lines over and over.
I smile when I remember the fishing contests as
they placed their pumpkin seed blue gills side by side
for the judging.
I see their excitement as the bobbers disappear
again, and they expect to see old "pud" thrashing
about at the end of their line.
I watch the blue heron softly glide to a landing
beside the water's edge then begin his search for just
the right silver minnow.
The greatest comfort of all is not just the time that
I am loving, but knowing my time is because He has
time to be there with me.

CHAPTER 22

TRAVELING DAZE

Twenty years from now you will be more disappointed by the things that you didn't do than by the ones you did do. So throw off the bowlines. Sail away from the safe harbor. Catch the trade winds in your sails. Explore. Dream. Discover.

--Mark Twain

The first time I saw a license plate that read, "We are spending our kids' inheritance," I smiled.

My travel adventures, until I turned fifteen, were mainly trips within three counties, McLean, Daviess, and Ohio. In 1960, I traveled by bus, with my future husband's family, to Pensacola, Florida. That same year, a friend of the family invited me to attend my brother's Navy graduation at Great Lakes, Illinois. Those ventures whetted my appetite to explore new territory.

When the boys were young, we would go to a finance company to borrow money for a trip to Florida, Smoky Mountains, Colorado or any place we could be together and find adventure. We always paid the note in time to borrow for our next trip. As teens, the boys found other interests and the vacations became less costly. Then the grandchildren arrived, and we started the cycle again. Thankfully, we no longer had to depend on our finance company, but we began spending our extra money, thus the apropos license plate. We are rich with memories and stories to help us smile if we are faced with the confinement that old age sometimes brings.

My first exposure to email, facebook and other forms of quick communications made me cringe. I read pages that had been written without the slightest attempt to use correct grammar or punctuation, not to mention letters heaped together which made no sense to me. I felt my years of teaching English/Writing just fade away. I still do not know many of the letters that are put together to a form hurried messages, that is probably best. However, I have found myself taking advantage of compiling my thoughts together quickly and without paragraph form.

The following is a compilation of emails sent during our most recent travels.

WEST TRIP 2008

Well, this ole country girl finally realized a 30 year dream. Tom Jr. flew to Los Angeles and took me to The Price is Right. We did not reach the stage, but we were so excited, we hardly noticed. What an experience! I won't bore you with too many details. I will tell you that if you ever get a chance to go, please do. We sat on the sidewalk from 4: am until 6: am. We then had 45 minutes to check out of our room and have breakfast. We spent 10 hours inside the CBS studio with a bunch of idiots just like us. Saw a woman who sported, and I mean sported, a set of size 50DDDDDDD breasts. She wore a size 10 top over a size 30 A bra. On the other side of us was a man who did not want to be there, so he sauntered around in front of me until I finally poked him in the back to move him along. He cooperated the rest of the day. Tom Jr. was mortified. The slow guy just laughed and said he was used to being pushed around by women. Sorry I have so many tales of the day, but I will spare you some. One poor man was drunk at 4, trying to get sober at 7, coming down slowly by 10, sick by 11, on the front row telling folks how to bid by holding up three fingers for every bid. One couple tried to stuff an old lady under a low bar behind her bench. She became wedged, and I know she has splintered bones in her shoulder and hip. I almost broke mine twisting and turning myself as I watched them try to extract her in one piece. A very pretty, young girl, who forgot she was wearing a dress, tried to crawl under her bar.

I was so sorry Tom Jr. had to witness that. We finally entered the studio, the crowd (Ardie too) was so worked up, that we danced, sang, screamed, etc., until Drew appeared. Then we were off the wall! So much fun. And, yes, the models are beautiful. The prizes are great. Drew was so good with the crowd during the breaks. He glanced at me and I smiled. I kept sticking out my front and pointing to my shirt. Tom caught me and made me stop. Tom also told me to stop trying to find myself in the monitor. I couldn't help myself. So if you all get a chance to watch on July 2nd, we are in the 3rd row back behind the contestants. We were wearing white shirts with blue writing. Just look for the bushy headed wild woman who is always staring at the ceiling. Do not look for the DDDDDDDDD bra lady. I mean it. Look for me. Bye and love to all.

WEST TRIP 2008

Hello fellow travelers, I really feel as if you all are with us sometimes. Again, we have Wi-Fi most places, but not very speedy when we are in the hollows (they call them valleys out here). We made it to Pahrump, NE, Thursday 26th, 08. But, I must add, not without incident. Wednesday night, we were awakened by a loud noise from the sky. Then large spotlights began dancing around our trailer. Ty and I peered out the window and saw a helicopter hovering above us. It flew away a few yards and then came back. Now, if you are wondering what my Tom Sr. and Jr. were doing! They were sleeping! I tried to tell Ty that they were probably from Edwards Air Base and just practicing something. That worked for a minute until I glanced behind our home and there stood a policeman, holding a big dog in one hand and a gun in the other. I told Ty to keep his head down; he didn't know where to put his head, and I didn't know where to tell him. I hurried to the living room, awakened Jr. He asked if Dad knew where his gun was and went back to snoring. Ty was my shadow by now. We looked out all the windows and discovered that the park was surrounded by police cars. My shadow and I stumbled back upstairs to awaken Sr. He was, by this time, peering out his window. Ty wanted to turn on the TV to see if we were on 'Cops.' We watched this scene for about an hour. During this time I thought I saw 3 ax murderers, at least 4 rapists, and numerous drug dealers, all of whom were hiding under our truck, our picnic table, or the trailer.

Finally, everyone left us. We have no idea for

whom they were searching or if they found anyone. By 1:30 am, we were back in bed, Sr. comfortable with half of the bed, Ty on top of me as I hung to the straps on the side of the mattress. Then as we came out of Vegas last night, suddenly sirens screamed, and lights flashed as a police vehicle pulled up behind us. Tom Jr. was driving us in his rental car. We were only a few blocks from our home and traveling about 15 mph. Lord, I thought, here we go again. Tom started reaching for his billfold, when another cop car sped by us lights flashing. The police never came to our car so we drove on to the park. I know most of you have been to Vegas, but our last visit was in 1983, so we were thrilled out of our wits to see the lights. Ty said it was like a dream. We went to Circus-Circus where they have a whole city inside the building. Tom Jr. is taking Ty back today to play laser tag and other things he will enjoy. As we were leaving the casino, Jr. dropped $20 into a machine and won $108.00. The winnings came out in big heavy coins. We couldn't find a container, so he just stuffed them in his pockets and held up his pants as he went to cash them in. I thought I would just drop in $20 since I had planned to gamble $100.00 while in Vegas. I didn't know what to watch for on the screen or how to play. I just touched the button that said max bet. Suddenly, those big tokens began dropping from the machine. I just stood back and watched. It would pause for a second then drop some more. A crowd gathered, and I asked someone when it would stop, and he said when it paid off. It stopped after it had paid me $214.00. A lady brought me two big buckets.

I filled both of them and hurried to find Jr. He was

in line cashing his coins. When he saw me with a bucket full under each arm, he cracked up. Guess who bought breakfast? Well, I have done it again. Talked too much, sorry. Guess we will fish today. Hope I don't get caught in the sprinklers again. Thursday, as I was relaxing and fishing, I heard a funny noise beside me and glanced around just in time to see these black spigots rise from the grass. My mind was in high gear, but my rear wouldn't co-operate. By the time I had reeled in my rod, and grabbed my chair, I was wet, wet, wet ! A lady watched my struggle and then said, 'At least you got cooled off.' Boy was she brave.

Love to all from Pahrump, Nevada

WEST TRIP 2008

Hello my fellow travelers, we have arrived in Loveland CO. Our reunion with my cousin was so neat. We had so much to share. Three more cousins will be here for a dinner tomorrow. We are going to a gravesite tomorrow and take Tommy to a western wear store. Snow was lying on the ground and mountains near Loveland Pass today. It snowed for a while then turned to rain for about ten minutes. This is the first rain we have seen for 30 days. Tommy has been ill. He is much better now, but we think he may have gotten food poisoning from a salad. He did not eat for days. I just hope it was not a stomach virus that is contagious. Heading for Kansas on Thursday. Tommy will be 66 tomorrow. When we return, I really don't expect any of you to treat me any differently just because I am now a TV star. NO! Don't even ask; I will not sign autographs...unless you really insist. I am so sleepy. Going to bed. Big day tomorrow. Sure do love all of you.

Alaska Log 1
June 10th, 2009

What an exciting day for us. Waited 49 years. Rod and the boys came up to the trailer looking for breakfast. I officially started my vacation 2 hours ago. Rod just told the boys he would go home and fry them some hotdogs. I should have felt guilty, but didn't. Hope to take all of you with us in words. Love to ya. Talk to you in a few thousand miles and hopefully smiles.

Bye from Bardstown, KY.

Alaska Log 2
June 10th, 2009

Well this ole country couple is still so excited. We have landed safely at O'Hare. I said landed safely, but we had a jar to our guts and nerves as we rode to our gate. Someone pulled a huge baggage cart in front of us and our pilot had to brake suddenly to save our right wing. I'm ok! We had a 5 hour wait in Chicago, and I had not eaten breakfast. There are 52 restaurants in the airport. We squeezed into a place called The Skybox. It is a sports bar that has 26 TV's. We decided to share a large appetizer plate. I always thought share means share. I gave Tommy all the calamari because I don't care for it. I thought that would leave me a larger portion of the wings, strips, fries. Didn't happen. When he reached for the last strip and asked if I wanted the rest of my dip, I thought about breaking his finger, but I didn't want to start our trip in a medical center or jail. So, as we roamed toward our departing gate, I stopped at McDonald's where I picked up some hamburgers for the long ride. The plane was delayed for twenty minutes so I ate one burger. A man knocked his suitcase over and hit my big toe, so I ate another burger. After boarding, we were scanning the folks as they boarded to see who would be sleeping with us. I looked up and there stood Davy Crockett. He had a full salt and pepper beard, rugged boots, a rawhide necklace with a bear tooth hanging from his neck, a cud of tobacco in his lower lip, and a sweet smile. He was my prince. For over six hours he occupied Tommy and me with his wildlife stories. He also gave us tips on where to eat and places to visit and a fishing guide. He is a wildlife hunting guide in AK and Wyoming. I ate another burger--they were so small. Then I noticed they had a picnic pack for sale for six dollars. I convinced Tommy that we should purchase two so that we could munch at our leisure. The picture showed, pepperoni, aged cheese, butter baked crackers, Amish bread, strawberry jam, almond maple butter, and a candy bar. Yum! When the attendant brought our "picnic" she handed me a container slightly larger than a Cracker Jacks box. I waited for the rest. Didn't happen. She took our twelve dollars smiled and departed. I ate another hamburger. I did turn toward the window to be discreet. Tommy ate the last burger for breakfast the next morning and even offered me half. I guess he felt bad about the appetizer meal. Yah right! I am including a couple of pictures I took as we landed. One looks like clouds around the mountains, but that is actually ice-called the Harding Ice Fields. It is so neat. Looks like frozen clouds. We love all. So glad to have you all along.

Alaska Log 3
June 12th, 2009

It is never dark here. The sun sets for about 3 hours, but it still is just like dusk at home. Tommy asks me 20 times a day if it is time to go to bed or to eat. We have seen no TV since we left. Today we toured Anchorage. We saw the world's largest collection of float planes. Many are docked on a lake where there are from 200 to 600 take-offs per day. There are more pilots in AK than any place in the world. Most of the teens learn to pilot by 13 and 14, and get their licenses when they are 16. The Wal-Mart is tiny, but they are building on. It had a few groceries, but no meal, just flour. Drinks are ten dollars a case. We took a trolley through town, listened to some local music, Tommy ate a reindeer sausage, and we were so tired. After returning to our RV, we rested then attended a little gathering at the rec hall. A gentleman made Irish stew and lemonade. He seasoned it with AK beer. It was delicious. A great magician performed. He asked for volunteers and I was very happy to help. I had a ball. Tommy just sat there trying to pretend he didn't know me. I really raked him over when we got home. There I am, my first performance as a professional magician helper, and he just stuck his nose in his stew and slurped away. Bless his heart; he is so bashful. A really wonderful singer followed "our" show. He could really play the guitar and sing all types of music. Tomorrow headed for Seward on Resurrection Bay. Still loving AK. Still loving you all. Still loving God.

Alaska Log 4

June 13th, 2009

Now on Resurrection Bay at Seward, AK. The Seward highway is one of the most beautiful drives I have seen. The mountains remind me of the green mountains in Vermont. We saw a mountain goat with her baby high up in the rocks. The sea lions and otters are playing in front of our camper. We went to a fish fry here at Miller's Landing. What a treat for Tommy. I am not a fish lover, but the blackened bass was good. Tommy had his fill of grilled salmon and smoked salmon dip. This is a real laid-back area. The tides are from 15 to 20 feet high so the view changes twice a day. The owner of this place looks like a drunken sailor from the book Treasure Island. I have to pay two dollars an hour for internet here so I am quick on the draw when I sign on. Still no tv. I think Tommy is in withdrawal. I'm ok, I read from my Kindle. I am so surprised to see so few churches here. We sure miss our church family in Island. Jennie say hi to my class. Love to all. Will send more pics later.

Alaska Log 5
June 14th, 2009

Slept late. Made a skillet breakfast of new red potatoes, fresh mushrooms, chopped onions, fried turkey breast, sautéed in butter and topped with Swiss cheese. Good! Yum! Watched the sea lions and otters and eagles enjoy the bay waters. Some folks are sailing, some are kayaking, some are cruising, some are digging for razor clams, some are fishing; we're just watching so far. Ravens awakened us this morning as they walked across our roof. Rained some today, so we just stayed close to home and ate and slept. So far we have counted 7 dogs that they call sea dogs here. Chocolate lab, border collie, Irish setter, some that are white with black spots. They are so sweet. They play with all the kids and go out on the fishing trips. I have us scheduled through 22nd of June now. I think we are going to need a good paying job for each of us so we can afford to fly home. Heading into Seward to see some wildlife and empty our tanks tomorrow. Tuesday we are going on a cruise to see the whales, ice fields, and other wonderful sights. They are supposed to feed us breakfast and lunch, but I am taking a burger just in case I need more nourishment. Love to All.

Alaska Log 6

June 15th, 2009

Chilly again today. We toured Seward, which took all of 10 minutes. It is a cute little bay town. We left Miller's landing camp and are camping in the Seward Resurrection Bay Park. Toured Sea Life today. It is a rescue facility which was funded by the money AK received from the Exxon crude oil spill. It cost 37 million to build. The sea animals and birds were so unique to this KY couple. I learned the differences between seals and sea lions. We enjoyed a beautiful exhibit of the bottom of the Bering Sea. We are fishing just off the sea the 18th. Lunch was at The Mariner restaurant. I am determined to eat some King Crab, but each time I look at the menu, I shudder! King Crab dinner was $38.00, but I could have ordered it as a side for $34.00. I ordered a BLT with bean soup. Tommy finally ate some Halibut. Said it was very tasty, just not as good as grouper in Florida. Next stop, Safeway for milk. Oh my goodness!! I am still in shock. I am so glad we stocked up on staples before we left Anchorage. Green bell peppers are $2.39 each; tomatoes are $4.59 a pound, drinks from $10 to $13 per case. One package of two Twinkies is $1.39. People were actually shopping in that store. People can fuss about Wal-Mart all they want to, but this is a town with one major store and it is only a hundred miles from Wal-Mart. I know it does not cost that much more to bring goods here. Guess what I bought? Nothing! Tommy bought a case of Pepsi and some peanuts at the cost of $19.00. The bottled water is very reasonable though. I even see people filling jugs from the mountain waterfalls. The tap water is very cold and good. I tried to get Tommy to just drink water, but he is already in withdrawal from TV. He finally found one station tonight from Chicago. I asked him what was on and he didn't even know. He was just enjoying the sound. Lordy.

We have not seen a franchise restaurant since we hit the Kenai. I knew I should have loaded up from McDonald's dollar menu. I am not complaining; I enjoy cooking in our little camper and the few times we have eaten out have been great.

I won't have net until the 17th. So I am sending a few logs at the same time. Again, if I am bugging anyone, just block me; I won't be upset.

Love and peace to all.

Alaska Log 7

June 16th, 2009

We have been to almost heaven. The boat picked us up at 8:30 a.m. They advertised a breakfast snack and a healthy lunch. Snack and healthy didn't sound too filling to me, so I stashed some cheese, crackers, and bananas in our bag. The boat has a capacity of 150, but there were only about 30 folks traveling. So glad. After a brief stop at Fox Island to drop off some kayakers, our adventure began. Sea otters first. When the captain announced the otters, everyone hurried to our side of the boat. We were in 900 ft of water, so I was not happy for all those people rushing to one side. I'm ok. Big boat. A little later I saw a whale come up like a torpedo. I did not say a word; I didn't want the stampede. Our next stop was at an island covered with sea lions. Then on to humpback whales, fin whales, and killer whales. We saw puffins. I'll send pictures too. Then we went through a bunch of ice, and I was scared. There were chunks as large as a truck, but we had to go through it to get to a glacier and waterfall. So, so beautiful! I will send pics of Puffins and whales later. Breakfast was fruit and rolls. Not bad. Then came lunch. The first thing I saw was a little bag of carrots and a granola bar. Then I found a chicken roll-up. I was pleased with both meals, and then they baked fresh cookies for us later. This is the 49th state we have visited. I could live here if all of you precious people would move with us. Well, I guess I can forget that; we don't draw enough money to buy Tommy's Pepsi. I'll sign off for now. I am going to fry chicken wings for supper. I'll eat an extra one for you Eugene. Love and peace to all!

Alaska Log 8
June 17th, 2009

Up early today. My sweet sister called at five. She forgot the time difference. We are moving down coast later this morning. I think I forgot to tell you all that I will not be shaving the backs of my legs for some time. I'm ok. Story! Tommy is cold natured; he is on blood thinner. I am hot natured with sufficient insulation. He packed a small electric heater in a suitcase just to be sure he could stay warm. Lordy! I was pleased with the heater because I could sneak to adjust it or turn it so it faced him, not me. Then he found the furnace controls for the RV. My seat of choice in the RV has been at the booth table. One morning, as I worked at my computer, he fired up the furnace. One doesn't quickly rise from one of these seats. It seems that the furnace and vents are under these booth seats. This is an Alaskan furnace too. Each naked leg rested in front of a vent. The initial blast almost blew my legs off the floor, I tried to lift both legs and almost broke both toes as I kicked Pepsi cases stored under the table--all the while I was scrambling to extract myself from the booth and yelling, "Turn it off, turn it off." Tommy yelled back that he would after he tried it out. He didn't realize that at this point I had possibly two broken toes, singed hairs, and almost a wet booth. We have the vents aimed differently now, and when he fires up, he yells "watch the legs!" Now set up in Homer. I washed two loads of laundry today. The washers were $ 3.25 a load and dryers were $2.00 a load. Packing for our fishing trip tomorrow. Love All.

Alaska Log 9

June 18th, 2009

Lordy, my goodness, wow, awesome, all apply to our fishing trip. We packed our lunch of turkey, chips, boiled eggs, drinks and fruit, called a taxi and off we went at 6:30 a.m. There were four men, including Tommy, on the boat. Sea otters lay on their backs with babies on their bellies, huge birds joined us, and an occasional whale snorted at us. We began fishing early and things were quiet for a while. Then the action started. My first one weighed "only" about 12 pounds so we tossed it back. Since we could keep only two each, we hoped for larger Halibut. I guess we threw back about two hundred pounds of fish. Made me sick. Tommy caught a huge skate that is dangerous so I didn't get a good picture of it. It weighed about 60-70 pounds. I caught the second largest fish on the boat which was only 35 pounds. The tops was 62 pounds. Tommy and I together netted 80 pounds and was able to send 40 one pound filets home. The sea food markets here charge $14.75 per pound of Halibut. It was another God sent day for us. My arm is so sore that I can hardly type. For those who watch " The World's Deadliest Catch," the captain of our boat used to work on Deadliest Catch ship called the Time Bandit. Some of the boats dock here at Homer and two of the captains live here. Their names are Johnathan and Andy Hillstrand. I am sleeping in tomorrow. When we go to bed, it is daylight. And when we awaken it is daylight. So strange. Love and Peace to all.

Alaska Log 10
June 19th, 2009

Stayed in bed late today. Our day started with a wonderful sight. I was preparing to put our pork chops and eggs on the table when Tommy yelled to come look out the window. There walking right beside our trailer was a moose and her baby. If I had been outside, Tommy would still be searching for me. The baby's hips were taller than I am. I didn't get a picture because I wasn't dressed and I wouldn't go outside. They just ambled by as if they were in the forest. I'm so happy to see these sights. We went shopping and sightseeing at Homer. We visited the Time Bandit shop today. Bought signed pictures for the grandkids. The captain, Johnathan, is supposed to meet us in the morning for some pictures. As we were driving down the road, there were more moose. I am so amazed. We ate at a restaurant on the Homer Spit, a 4 mile strip of land that juts out into Cook's Inlet. We laughed but wanted to cry. Tommy ordered local oysters on the half-shell as an appetizer. Then he ordered a sampler platter of prawns, red salmon, and halibut. Oh my goodness. He got 6 tiny oysters, 2 prawns, a piece of halibut about the size of a cell phone, and a piece of salmon the same size. I got 5 fried oysters and slaw. The bill was $59.00. Again, we expected some of these prices, but it is still a shock sometimes. I found some reasonable prices on some sale items at Safeway. Then when we reached the car, I discovered that they had not given me the discounts. Took me 20 minutes to get my $15.00. For anyone who smokes: cigarettes are $7.89 a pack. Winstons are $66.90 a carton. I hope you folks realize that I am not whining. I am just in wonder at the differences in our Ky and other places.

Getting ready to board the Marine Highway ferry at 10 a.m. tomorrow. We have a berth with all facilities both ways. Should arrive at Kodiak Island about 7:30 p.m. The ferry has full meal service and entertainment on board. I'll send some more pics soon. Love all!

Alaska Log 11
June 20th, 2009

Taxi picked us up a 9 a.m. off to catch the ferry. We stopped on the way to see if Johnathan, the captain, was home. He was still with his boat which had a diesel leak. Hey, we may see that part on TV. We will return to Homer Tuesday and will stop by his place again. We may try out The Otter Room, which is a bar where the crab guys hang out. The ferry is carries 42 vehicles and 174 people. It was only four stories high, but big by my standards. For lunch we ate a cold pork chop, cheese, crackers, and drinks. I walked by the dining room and sniffed several times. So we decided to try their supper. Great, great meal. Tommy had roast beef with gravy, baked potato, mixed vegetables. I had jalapeno chicken cheese soup, a philly with potatoes. Yum! Our little cabin on board was really a little cabin. Had four bunk beds and a bath. We whale watched for a while, then snoozed for an hour or so. I loved the ship rocking as I dozed. Whales were snorting all during the trip. Puffins glided across the water and porpoise jumped as if performing at Sea World. Tommy made friends with a native Alaskan, who is a retired fisherman. He had lots of information about AK. The shuttle was waiting at the port. Had an uneventful three block ride to our motel. We were ready to rest for the night. There is no air conditioner in any of the rooms. But, the temp has not been over 72 since we arrived. Good Night from Kodiak, AK!

Alaska Log 12
June 21st, 2009

Nice room, slept well. Big breakfast furnished by the motel. Then we found another almost heaven. The island has only 100 miles of paved roads. Well, some are not well paved. But I would walk on glass to see this beautiful place. I took pictures, but they will not do justice to the real thing. We went bear hunting too. When we left town, there were no services. I forgot to pee. Finally, I had to tell Tommy to find some place so that I could go. I was so afraid that a bear's cold nose would nuzzle my naked butt cheek, or worse, use one for an appetizer, that I made Tommy leave the door open, and I leaned against the bumper so I could see three ways. Of course, Tommy had to sneeze. I did not say a word to him; I was too weak. We saw huge bald eagles on the beach and drove to the end of a gravel road where people actually live in a jungle. Found a Wal-Mart here. It was so tiny. I bought some socks, but they only had a few groceries. We did find a place to buy some late-night snacks. Lordy, we love this state. No, we could not live here. I just read in the motel handbook that if a loud siren blasts, we are to head for high ground because that is a tsunami warning. It reminded me of the boat warnings and drills after we were on board. They showed us the proper way to abandon ship, just in case. Reminds me of Bill Cosby not wanting to say the prayer:

Now I lay me down to sleep,

I pray the Lord my soul to keep,

If I should die!!!!!!!!

"Oh no," he said, "I was not about to go to sleep then."

Well, I felt about the same, except I couldn't get off the boat or the island. I'm ok. Love to all.

Alaska Log 13
June 22nd, 2009

I have never had gravy and biscuits made with pure, sweet butter until now. Yum! We drove around looking for that ole Kodiak bear again. Didn't happen. I saw stump bears, bush bears, rock bears, and tree bears. Every time I spotted a brown bush, stump, rock, or tree, I thought I saw teeth snarling, claws bared and ready to attack, and one even waved at us. The Kodiaks were not wandering about. Tommy went shopping for pink lures for Florida. That man is going to spend us into the poor house! He has purchased caps for everyone, shirts for him, and of course he is still drinking those darn Pepsi's. Rod called to tell us that there had been an earthquake in Anchorage. We stopped at a visitor center and a lady showed us the quake, and told us that there had been a small one two miles from us. She said they are used to small ones though. She also said that Kodiak is setting on an ocean shelf that is slowing sliding into the waters. Lordly! We still had 3 hours before our ferry left. Found a fish and chips café for supper. Tommy had salmon, said it was very good. I am not a big fish eater, so I had chicken with some kind of delicious dip. The cook dipped both the fish and chicken into the same mixture. I loved it. I hurried Tommy to the ferry. We boarded at 4 and left at 6 p.m. The water was so smooth. The ferry stopped on the way back to Homer at a place called Port Lions. Amazed, just amazed that people live in such beauty, yet without constant contact with the outside world. The population of the borough of Kodiak is approx. 218. They dropped off a water truck, and a few people and cars. The only way in or out is by boat or plane. Most of the residents are Eskimo natives. The sea life played around the leaning wooden dock, kids hurried down to wave and watch. They have 74 inches of snow yearly. What beauty, what isolation. We took a ham, crackers and cheese snack, ate late and retired. Again, I slept like a baby being rocked in God's arms. The boat just swayed enough to be comforting. Arrived in Homer about 7:30 a.m.

Alaska Log 14
June 23rd, 2009

Set alarm so we could shower on the ferry. Called taxi and headed home. It was very cool here today. As soon as we arrived at the trailer, I saw Tommy nosing around. Sure enough, he was watching the truck load of fish parked at the rv office. He insisted that I go check the fish and the prices. The truck was loaded with Sockeye Salmon. He shipped 20 pounds home. We will be on the corner with a monkey and a tin cup. After doing the laundry, we went to the Spit to check on the boat captain from "Deadliest Catch." His secretary said she would call me when he arrived. She called and we went back to the Spit at 5 p.m. I had pictures made with him, and he signed more autographs for people back home. I asked him if I could kiss him on the cheek for my granddaughter. He smiled and said, " May I kiss you?" I'm ok. He had to kiss me four times before the gentleman using my camera could get it right. The other ladies were going wild. I think my cheek is scratched from his tough whiskers. Finally, Tommy spoke up and Johnathan asked if he was my husband. Johnathan said, "oops, we'll be finished in a moment." Life is sweet!! Leaving for Cooper Landing tomorrow. XOXOXO

Alaska Log 15
June 24th, 2009

We made it to Cooper Landing. We did not find the elusive Kodiak. I really wanted to see the largest bears on earth, but I'm sure they were peering at us. I learned that the Kodiak is the same species as the grizzly and brown bear. They became isolated on the island and grew larger than their cousins. We are between the Kenai and Russian River. When we arrived, the office was closed for lunch so we parked in our reserved spot. Tommy went to bed, and I ventured to the office to pay. I didn't hear about the numerous bears in the area until I spoke with the hostess. They even take the trash bins up at night so the bears won't raid them. Well, this missy hurried, as fast as a arthritic cripple can hurry, back toward the RV. I listened for any sound other than my breathing, Suddenly, a bush behind an RV started to shake violently. Lordy! I took a few quick steps and looked toward the bush again. There stood a stupid, stupid, stupid, man who evidently was trying out a new fly rod. He was jerking on the line, which was entwined in the bush. I hope he never catches a fish with that darn rod. I'm ok. I think. As I am writing this, we are waiting for a shuttle to take us to the Kenai for a two hour raft ride. The man said that even though I am old and scared, I will be safe. We'll see! He said we will see salmon spawning, eagle nests, bears, moose, and wild flowers. I'm ready?

Hello, we are back and tired. This state is magical. The sights are so new, the air so clean, the water so cold, the Alaska Thunder potato chips are delicious, and the people so friendly. A small young man from

Wisconsin picked us up for the raft trip. I say small because I wanted a large person to guide us in case the river current or a bear bothered us. I asked him if he had been trained in bear combat, and he said he had been trained to run. We rode for 13 miles down the Kenai and hit the Russian where the salmon are spawning. There were at least 100 bald eagles on the route. The shores were lined with pink wild roses. The huge seagulls ferociously fought over the salmon carcasses . Still have not spotted a bear. I may have to come back to Kentucky to see one. When we hit the Russian river, there were hundreds of anglers lining the banks. I took pics. They were all ages and sizes standing to their waists in the water.

I have been having difficulty with my left knee. I have arthritis from head to toe. Well, it finally kicked in today. I am in so much pain that I cannot walk. Keeping Tommy busy. He is even waiting on me so I don't have to walk much.

Love to all.

Alaska Log 16
June 25th 2009

Off to the hospital, can't stand, can't walk, didn't sleep until Tommy doped me up with one of his pain pills. Tommy chose the smallest wheel chair in the state. I am not going to criticize him. He has been so concerned and helpful. But, I squeezed in without much problem. My knee was hurting so badly that even a little hip rubbing from the plastic seat that was hitting the wheel was tolerable. We spent the day in the emergency room. They put me in the pediatric room. For four hours, Tommy rocked in the Mommy chair, I hung out -literally- in the wheel chair as we both stared at a huge, white polar bear bed. It had big blue eyes , thick lips, and medicine drawers under its stomach. I looked at it so long, that I'm not sure that I even want to see an Alaskan bear now. I told Tommy that I would draw the line if they ask me to climb onto that bed. It seems that Tommy and I bring out the worst in emergency rooms. They were piled up waiting for service. A man had presented who was covered in asbestos. They shut down the ER. There was a three car accident when an elderly lady with bright orange hair bounced on a curb and took out two parked cars. Both occupied. The lady with the orange hair looked to be about 200 and blind. Bless her heart; she would have to be. Please understand, I am not making fun of her. I am just stating facts. She was in the stall next to me, and she demanded attention all day long. One person in the other car was injured, not seriously. Later, as they tried to dismiss the elderly lady, I kept wondering if someone was picking her up. If not, I wanted to be dismissed first to make my get-away.

I wanted relief and was hoping for a shot in my knee, but they cannot do that in the emergency room. The doctor checked for blood clots too. He said that they see lots of blood clots in people because of the long flights to here. Gary came in with the dope, and I tried to tell him that I didn't need much, but I was hurting so badly that I swallowed it all. An aspirin makes me sleepy, so imagine me with 800 mil of Motrin and two Percocets on an empty stomach. Gary, a sweet and caring R.N., took me to x-ray, he started to push, then asked me if the brakes were on-- they were not. Gary's going to live. Maybe. He asked me what that loud clicking was at the wheel. I told him to shut up and drive. He was fluffy too. We both got so tickled, he could hardly get me to x-ray. The staff was so great. One doc for 12 patients. One wanting to punch a bear in the snout, one wanting attention every minute, another faking back pain so he could get drugs, and then they hear that Michael Jackson is dead. We were next to the nurses' station. It was like being in a four chair beauty shop. Tommy couldn't rest for nosing. The tests showed severe arthritis, some fluid somewhere, and lots of inflammation. Doc referred me to an orthopedic doc next door. He cannot legally administer a steroid shot.

Tommy wanted to know if I felt like going shopping. Shoot, I could have bought out Wal-mart the way I felt and laugh about it.

When we arrived at the store, I wanted to drive the electric cart. He looked nervous. I don't think he wanted another er visit. All went well until I ran out of power. We made it fine though; he pushed me as I steered. He wanted me to run over people like he does driving, but I would put on my brake and chock him up. We exchanged a few words and went home where I passed out for the night. I'm ok. Tommy is tired.

Good Day from Anchorage.

Alaska Log 17
June 26th, 2009,

Off to the doc for a knee shot. I am very pleased with the medical facilities and personnel here in Anchorage. I was reading my Kindle when the PA came in to evaluate me. He wanted to talk about it more than my knee. We laughed and enjoyed some talk about our lives, Then doc came in; he spotted my Kindle and here we go. He wanted to look at it and talk about it. I asked them if they remembered why I was there. Again, we visited for a while. They were a hoot to talk to, and not at all bad on the eyes. When the doc told me that the PA would administer the shot, I asked why. I was happy with his care. The shot was painless. I am so much better. They wanted me to fly back for knee replacement. I don't think so.

Received some good news from home. Anthony, Rod's 15-year-old, was sent to Lexington for his migraine headaches. The docs said his neurological exam showed that he had nothing else causing the problem. They said that sometimes puberty causes these severe headaches. He is now taking preventative meds that are working. Rod's surgeon prescribed new stockings which are keeping him more comfortable.

We went shopping at a store called Fred Myers. Finally, a store I liked. It is huge! The store reminds me of a huge one in Louisville.

We are back where we started in the Golden Nuggett RV park. Tommy has gone to the rec hall to hear some music and eat some corn stew. I am trying to download some pics.

Leaving tomorrow for a park outside Wasilla where we are hoping to visit Sarah Palin. Then on to

Valdez to see the pipeline.

Thanks for your prayers and I appreciate your allowing me to share our wonderful trip. I will try to send some pics today.

Love you all.

Alaska Log 18
June 27, 2009.

In the boonies, in the boonies. I think it is called Glacier Mountain. Today we visited Wasilla. It is a very clean town built around a large lake. Sarah lives on the lake in a $550,000 home designed by Todd. We plan to go back by as we return to Anchorage. RV park we are in has cold mountain spring water. All the tap water in AK is cold and good. This is especially cold and tastes so pure. I filled my bottles before we left. As I was doing my laundry, I sat on a little porch looking toward a mountain. I spotted a white spot moving. I was a Dall sheep. The next morning, Tommy saw two hanging on the rocks. I made a pork and mushroom stew for supper. Tommy is not much for stews or soups so he has Spam, and cheese and peach pie. We tried to watch a little TV, but all the talk was about that Michael Jackson. I'm about to vent, so delete me from here. What in the hell has that person done to cause people to fawn over him. I enjoyed Elvis Presley; I used to enjoy George Jones before he lost his voice. I was sorry when Elvis died. I will be sorry when George Jones dies. But I do not worship either of them. I did cry when Mother Teresa died. Many people, especially children, lost a champion human being. What is wrong with people who expend so much God-given energy to grieve over the loss of someone who has made such an insignificant contribution to mankind. His family will grieve, his close loved ones will grieve, but, when strangers stand on the street and scream for him or fly thousands of miles to pay tribute to him, they have to be still cranking their rope. I have bad news for them; I don't think their engine will ever start.

Sorry, I am just full again. Sometimes I get that way. Heading for Valdez Sunday.

Alaska Log 19

June 28th, 2009

Just caught Tommy busy on the phone and turned on the air conditioner for the first time since we have been here. It is 73*, but the sun is beaming down on the trailer. I am always sad to leave each beautiful place we stay, but I know that we are just headed for another one. The drive today was astounding. We saw sheep, black bear, glaciers and tons of waterfalls. The bears were just black dots moving around on legs, but that was almost close enough for me. I guess there must be thousands of waterfalls from the ice melts and the glacier melts. Driving along the Alaskan pipe line was even exciting for us. Valdez is the shipping port for all the oil from Prudhoe Bay. I am so in love with all the wildflowers. I have a book which I plan to use to identify them. The natives say that everything here grows large and fast because of the short growing time. With all the daylight most plants just thrive. This is a very small town. I will not go to a restaurant here. It is at the end of the road so I know they will see tourist all over my KY t-shirt and want to rake in the dough. That's ok. I still love to cook. I must cook the rest of our chicken wings, two roasts, and a steak before the 8th of July. I made Tommy some fresh pork sausage this week. Found the seasoning and just added a little southern flavor. Tasted great. After I send this, I will try to send more pics. Thanks again for coming along. Good Night from Valdez, AK

Alaska Log 20
June 29th, 2009

I am writing this on Monday evening. Before I start on today's events, I have a confession to make. I decided I did not want to cook last night, so, yes, we went to a restaurant. I have been waiting for a good time to eat some King Crab. The time was right last night. Tommy had beer-battered halibut, and I had the crab. Don't ask me what it cost. My fingers will not be able to punch the keys. It was delicious, but really not any better than the King Crab that Tom Jr. buys for me at Sam's Club. As I ate, I thought of Tommy's Dad. They traveled with us often, and the first time we ate at a seafood diner and I had crab from the buffet, Dad was so embarrassed when I returned with my plate. He had never seen crab legs before. He relaxed after looking around and seeing that I was not the only crab glutton in the restaurant. After that, every time we traveled, Dad would always tell Tommy to stop at a place where I could get my "big crawfish legs" to eat. We miss them so much when we see something this wonderful. Today started with us wondering where we may stay tonight. There are not many parks between Valdez and Fairbanks. I guess you folks get tired of our constant praise of Alaska, but we just feel as if this is surreal sometimes. When we topped a mountain today to be presented with another wonder, Tommy said he felt as if these sights are not even real. We enjoyed the cruises on Prince William Sound, our fishing trip on Cooks Inlet, rafting the Kenai, and Russian Rivers, and our ferry ride in the Pacific. Loved the whales, porpoise, puffins, seals, otters, fish , etc. But, the interior of

Alaska has wowed the socks off us. Alaska is referred to by sections. I hope I am not offending anyone with this geography lesson, but I didn't know this until I started planning our trip. We have toured the South Central extensively. Hit one section of the Bush, which is Kodiak, and now we have entered the Interior. Folks who live here, or have been here, tell us that the best is yet to come at Denali. I'm not sure my eyeballs can stand much more. Saw another moose today. I love to see them lope along. They bounce as if they are on a trampoline. Some of the roads here have frost heaves. Deane and Millie warned us. LuAnn and Tony gave us some good advice too. But, you won't believe things until you are faced with them. When you have been on a road for two hours that causes you to either slide the seat out of you britches or bounce knots on your head, you do not want to look up and see a sign that says " rough roads next 2 miles." We just looked at each other and said, "Oh Lord!" I know one thing for sure, if a mother-to-be is ready to deliver, she needs to venture out on the Richardson Highway. I guarantee her, that baby will be crowning before she reaches Delta Junction. I even thought I may deliver a few times today. The jars and jerks and jostles did not take away from our love of the land. Didn't affect our appetite either. We consumed a twenty pack of jerky sticks that we had purchased while visiting Rod (hey Anthony we sneaked this pkg by you), and bag of Alaska Thunder chips (my favorite), and a few Pepsi's. We are at Delta Junction, just past the Greely Army Base. Tommy has been so enamored with the pipe line. He has friends who worked on it. We have followed it for many miles

from Valdez. I'll send pics. Good Night from Delta
Junction, AK XOXOXO

Alaska Log 21
June 30th, 2009

Well, we had an oops day. I thought I had been jarred and jostled before. But, I received a major jolt today. As we turned left into a service station, a man and lady in a Chevy dually hit us in the left rear. When the RV stopped moving, I looked at Tommy and asked him what in the world he had run over. Something had hit my arm and side. I glanced at the floor and realized the TV was lying beside me. The man had tried to pass us even though we had our signal on. We had just pulled out of a side road and was moving slowly. Most people do not want to be behind a big box, so he just whipped around us. He told the trooper that he tried to pass us but didn't realize we were going to turn. Oops! No one was hurt. I think we will all be sore tomorrow. As we pulled away, a lime rolled from under Tommy's seat. I had to search for my cooking oil and finally found it wedged under the oven. My pantry is white with flour. The folks who hit us were very kind. They have good insurance, rental place has insurance, and we have rental coverage. So, hopefully all will be covered. Tommy had to re-route the water spout so we could have water. The holding tank was destroyed. He repaired the lights so we have a blinker and brake light. The night stand on his side of the bed is twisted sideways. We put the chairs and fishing gear inside because there is no door to lock. It would have taken a day to transfer to another rental, so we are driving this one the rest of the trip. We get some curious stares, but that's fine. No one knows our names. The next person who asks me what happened, I am going to tell him/her that one of our Kentucky double-barreled shotguns misfired and blew out the back end. We're ok. There is farm land in Alaska. Big farms. I am surprised. We toured some of the agriculture area today. Fairbanks is more like home as far as landscape and prices. I bought tomatoes for $1.00 a pound. Tommy's Pepsi's were $7.98 a case. I am trying to cook up all the food in our freezer so we had plenty of chicken wings tonight with spinach and rice. We are off the Denali tomorrow. Maybe it will be an easier day. Good Night from Fairbanks, AK

Alaska Log 22
July 1st, 2009
Twenty-six years ago yesterday, Tom Jr. presented us with our first grandchild, Micheal Ryan Wilkerson. He is papaw's "little Bud." I guess one could say that we celebrated his birthday with a bang. That is my only corny one for today, promise. Last night, after we repaired the RV and took a few pictures, we were both exhausted. I started to arrange the bed when I noticed that light was coming in under Tommy's night stand. I peered closer only to discover that the gaping hole ran all the way under our bed. Lordy! I don't think they have snakes here, but I have seen chipmunks, squirrels, and other varmints scurrying around. I wanted to be brave and just not mention the hole because I knew that Tommy was tired. He found it. I tried to be brave again and tell him that there were no snakes, but he mentioned rats. That ended my bravado. He found a quilt, pulled out the drawer and stuffed it in the hole. All day he had to watch the quilt to be sure it didn't get sucked out the hole. What a hoot. Two old Kentuckians driving down AK 1, in an RV with a hole in its rear and a quilt flapping in the wind. We arrived at Denali without incident. Public vehicles can drive only 15 miles into the park. There were many tours we could have taken, but all were very lengthy and crowded. Our decision to just drive the 15 miles in was a good one. We got behind a tour bus and when someone spotted caribou , the bus screeched to a halt and I watched through the back window as the old coots scrambled on top of each other to get a photo. We two old coots behind the bus just started snapping pictures. Ate lunch in the

visitors' center parking lot. Tommy ate a half package of hotdogs, then looked at me and said , " I could eat another one." I told him to help himself; I wouldn't tell anyone! I had cold chicken wings. I didn't know those bags of Costco wings had so many pieces. Did not see Mt. McKinley until we drove around the north side of the park. I thought I had seen mountains until I saw this one. It is so high that it stays in the clouds three out of four days. So pretty. We are at Trapper Creek for the night. I have no net tonight, so will have to send email from Wasilla Thursday. When we arrive in Wasilla, we are going to try to find Sarah again. The last time we went through, we were headed for Valdez and did not stay long. I think we will stay two days so I can get a perm and do some laundry. Hope to spend the fourth of July in Anchorage. Tommy is going salmon fishing while there. I'm going to pass on that one. I'm hot natured and love fishing, but I have my limits. Standing in ice cold mountain water, wearing waders, and dodging flies is beyond my limit. Love all of you. Good night from Trapper Creek, AK

Alaska Log 23
July 2nd, 2009

Someone told us that the state bird of Alaska is the mosquito. We brought plenty of spray, but until last night we had not needed it. I found an emaciated, short nosed one on my arm when we were in Homer. I laughed at it. Guess he spread the word, because they found us last night. We heard their music all night. I searched for a place they may be entering and found another hole beside the night stand. I stuffed it full so maybe they will stay out tonight. Saw another moose yesterday. It was so pretty as it loped along a lake shore. Couldn't find a empty space in Wasilla. I forgot about the holiday week-end. Found a different park here that had TV cable for Tommy, but we only stayed 22 minutes. What a dump. We are in Anchorage at The Golden Nugget again. A jazz bang is playing, serving soup and rolls tonight at the rec hall. Some people may have received an email from a "former" friend of mine named Paul. He is our neighbor and adopted son from LaBelle, FL. I emphasized the word "former" after he revised my scenario about our accident. He is a young rooster yet and thinks of us as old farts who shouldn't be driving. No more nice Ky meals for our un-adopted son. Have actually had the air on the last two days. The temps are in the 70's. Love to all.

Alaska Log 24
July 3rd, 2009

Slept late this a.m. Didn't have any mosquito music to sleep by. Last night we attended a jazz session presented by the University of Alaska, Anchorage jazz band. I am not a jazz fan, but they were great. Kind of brought back memories of when I played the trumpet in our marching band--a few years ago! Not that I could have ever reached the high notes these two players belted out. One played his horn through the side of his mouth. A local restaurant served broccoli and chicken soup-yum. We washed clothes last night and took some more flower pictures. I am still in awe of their gardens and pretty flowers. Tommy ate a green apple and has the quick step. Traveled to my favorite store, Fred Myers, to purchase pepto. I can hardly get past the deli counter; the buggy wheels just seem to want to swivel in that direction. Goodness, what choices one has there. Their stuffed mushrooms are the size of baseballs. I was a good girl and just purchased some hot sauce, b-b-que sauce, cookies and ice cream. Tommy had nothing for lunch. I ate a coconut cream bar and some Nutter-Butter cookies. Tonight the Air Force brass band will be here. The park will serve chili. Saturday will be the usual 4th feast. The park will serve the meat and campers take the other dishes. I 'm going to hurry to eat because a bunch of people are going to play the bagpipes. I hate bagpipe music. They maybe will not play too long because Miss Anchorage, and another band playing folk music will be here also. I hope they are not dulcimers; I don't like those either. I will stay long enough to eat though. Then Bingo time Sunday.

We will be venturing around Anchorage and Wasilla, so we may miss some of these momentous events! Since this is Alaska's 50 year celebration, they are going all out with the celebrations downtown. There are fireworks stands blocks long. Hope the state doesn't burn down while we are here. Received a call from Tina today. She told us that Palin had resigned. Haven't had TV for days. We have been in Alaska only a few weeks and already the governor has quit, they have had two earthquakes, my leg gave in, and we've had a wreck. Thank goodness the missiles didn't fire, the mating bears have stayed in the mountains, and the volcano is resting. I have an appointment in Wasilla Tuesday to get a perm at the beauty shop where Sarah gets her updo. The news folks have converged here again; I hope they leave before Tuesday. Just in case they are still nosing around , and we get caught on camera, we will be easy to spot. Remember to look for a mutilated RV carrying a kinky-haired lady sporting a new "do." The time is 4:10 here; that means it is at least 8:10 for most of you all. Have a restful, sandman night and have a memorable 4th. Goodnight , and may God bless you all, from Anchorage, AK.

Alaska Log 25
July 4th, 2009

We just did absolutely nothing today. Tommy is feeling better after his stomach bout. But we were both content to rest, read and nap for a day. I made hot wings and potato salad for the supper at the park. Lots of good food served to celebrate the 4th. The men in kilts drove me crazy--not their legs--their music. I thought about tripping one to see if the story is true about what they do or do not wear underneath. Miss Anchorage did not show. Then a folk group played. We made more new friends at the meal. They are from Colorado, and those lucky folks said they were at the university purchasing a shirt for their daughter, when a gentleman asked them if they wanted to stay for the big event. They asked about the event and were told that Sarah Palin would arrive soon. They stayed for the event. Eat your heart out Fred Staples. The gentleman from Colorado said she was a doll even up close. He said he just wished he could have squeezed her. Lordy-old men! They will have the fireworks display here at midnight. Since it is light all night, they try to present them the earliest and with the most darkness. As I write this, it is 1:30 a.m. at home, but 9:30 p.m. here. The sun is still high, but will disappear for a few hours. It will remain light though because the sun is just over the horizon. When we arrive in Louisville Thursday about midnight, it will be the first time we have seen darkness since June 10th. I packed a flashlight. It has never been unpacked. Now isn't that a hoot. Heard from Ann Cobb this week. So sweet of her to write. She took us out to eat in Oklahoma about this time last year.

Jennie, I dreamed that Debbie and I presented you with a certificate for learning your ABC's. Some time I will tell you the whole dream. We're going to Wild Berry Park tomorrow and to the botanical gardens. Hope all of you had a happy, healthy, patriotic day. Sure miss everyone. We are both hating to leave this wonderland land, but are ready to see our family. Good night, God Bless.

Alaska Log 26
July 5th, 2009

Warm here again today. We went goat hunting down Seward Highway. They were taking a holiday too. I actually have the air on. It is 73* Filled up with propane and gas for the last time today. Tomorrow I will cook up the rest of our food. We will head downtown Anchorage for the last time, then travel to Wasilla Tuesday. Tommy took an off road today. It took us up through a mountain filled with rich homes. I can't imagine having the kind of money it takes to live like that. Notice I didn't say I want to live like that. I could enjoy living in a shack in the middle of the woods if Tommy would live there too. I know that, if we had millions, most of it would be shared with those in need. The remaining, I think I could use to keep Tommy in Pepsi's. We are both looking forward to getting home. Kentucky is not only beautiful, but I feel it is another gift to us from God. He knows I love to be barefoot and feel the dust between my toes. He knows I love to say, *you all.* He knows I want to be surrounded by real, honest, caring people, so he gave me my family, my church family and my great friends. He knows I love, beans, taters, cornbread, buttermilk, fried chicken, ham with red-eye, grits, mutton, poke greens, lemonade, ho-cakes, sliced tomatoes every meal, iced tea, turnips, fried cabbage, oh me, I must stop this, getting hungry. I should just say, "He knows." Played Bingo today too. Haven't played since March '08. I have a mystery. Last week as we were traveling the Glen Highway, we stopped at a roadside pull-off. There was one car there when we arrived. As we sat and talked a few moments, a man on a motorcycle pulled in front of us about 15 feet. He reached up to the rear view mirror of his bike and unscrewed it from the bike. He glanced around and walked into the wooded area and down a small hill, leaned over and placed the mirror beside a tree. He walked to his bike and turned back the way he had entered. Have no notion! We have had no TV for days, so if we need to know something, please write.

Alaska Log 27
July 6th, 2009

We're packed. Tommy had to buy another suitcase to bring home a few extras. I have been downloading some photos to send to folks who have no computers. Last night we had, you-can't-take-it-with-you soup. I cleaned out the fridge and cabinet to make a funny soup. I bragged on it as I cooked, hoping it would taste good. Don't even ask what was in it. I liked it; Tommy just ate silently. I am so airplane savvy now that I will not buy a picnic pack on the way to Chicago. Our plane departs at 8: a.m. so I will go to McDonalds and stock up on burgers and pies. I noticed that most McDonalds serve burgers all day now. If not, I will have a couple of their steak sandwiches--yum. Every time I go through security, they have to rummage my purse. That's ok as long as they leave my food alone. When boarding in June, I had to take Tommy's med bag through. Since he has a pacemaker and metal shoulder, he cannot go through the gate. They have to wand him. This lady wanted to know if that whole case was meds. I told her it was, but I wanted to pop her on her smirking smile too. I laugh at Tommy every time he has to almost undress before boarding. He says he wishes he could get hold of just one of those Osama nut heads. George Seymour may have solved the bike mirror mystery. He says some if the bikers hide things and give the coordinates to others so that they can try to find it with their GPS's. Better than anything I could imagine. Off to bed. Big day tomorrow. Love XOXO

Alaska Log 28
July 7th, 2009

So funny how some things happen. I just wanted to see the Palin home. We began circling Lucille Lake at Wasilla. Again, the roads up here are part of the surprises of AK. As we drove around Lake View Drive, the road became dirt. We are used to that by now. Tommy wanted to stop, but I was so curious as to what may be around the next corner. Turning the corner we spied an elderly lady working in her flower garden. We had driven right up into her yard. Tommy chocked up the RV and started backing out. I begged him to pull up and ask her where Sarah lives. The lady just stared at us then smiled and waved. After a few "Daddy" words, Tommy pulled forward and rolled down his window. I leaned across and asked her if we were near the Palin home. She looked serious for a moment, then said, "I am not a Sarah Palin fan." Oops! I just acted as if I had not heard her and smiled. She just smiled too, and told us the best shot we could get would be from her own lake front property. Then she insisted we drive down her road to the beautiful lake to take some photos. She even moved her truck so we could turn our heap around. We three began to socialize, and I almost forgot my appointment. The lady has been divorced 30 years, raised nine children, has 18 grandchildren, all of whom live within a few miles from her. What a quiet peaceful place she lives in. A moose gave birth a few weeks ago in her back yard, then ate all her broccoli to the ground. She asked us in for a visit. I love people like her. I did get a fair picture of the Palin home. It looks beautiful. I'm kinky! Yep, it is all cut off. I feel so head naked. The little girl who did my do was so cute and young. She spent lots of time with my stiff, old, grays. Even massaged my head for five minutes. Charged only $25.00. I haven't had a perm that cheap for years. I tipped her well. We talked about Sarah and her family. She said that the Palins are a really down to earth family. Said Todd had made their money working on the North Slope. A band is playing here tonight so Tommy will be happy. I think they are serving chili too. Leaving at 8 a.m. AK time. We won't be sitting together unless we can beg for the exit seats which have more leg room. I'll really have all the burgers to myself this time. If it is not too expensive, we may upgrade to first class if there are any empty seats at boarding. Tommy is still having shoulder pain since we took a jolt in the accident. Rod will pick us up at midnight Wednesday. Looking forward to hugging everyone. Good Night from Anchorage, AK

Alaska Log 29

July 9th, 2009

My Old Kentucky Home. Happy birthday to Tommy today. He is now 67 years old. He said I should remind Dillar that she had her 67th birthday 7 days ago. Rod, Tom, and Anthony picked us up at midnight. I was not happy with the Alaska Airlines plane landing in Chicago, but I was really unhappy when the AA commuter jet bounced onto the runway at Louisville. I'm ok. Tommy had so much debris to bring home that we had to pay extra for our baggage. I learn something new every day. I learned to not pack mustard in a checked bag. I tie-dyed one of my white shirts a dingy yellow. Most of my crackers are crumbs. Cheerios were hiding in shoes, underwear, hats, etc. When we gave Rod his Alaska hat, he asked if there were lots of sand in AK. There are plenty of sand and dirt roads, but the substance on his hat was cheerio and cracker dust. Two out of three of our bags were inspected after being checked. Evidently they didn't repack the way I had packed. Oh well, I didn't have to crush my crackers tonight when I made my squash casserole. Pam's garden is producing. Tommy ate well for supper. Had pickled cucumber/onions, squash casserole, breaded/fried spam, cob corn, and fresh lettuce. I want to thank everyone for allowing us to share our trip. I relived each day as I composed my emails. There were wonderful experiences that cause me to think of many of you. God bless all of you. Good Night from Bardstown, KY.

Tommy's Stroke
October 7th, 2009

We were in our travel trailer at Rodney's, our younger son, who lives near Bardstown, KY. His 15-year-old was to have 5 teeth extracted, and the other two sons had dental appointments, so we were there to help. Tommy reached toward a ceiling light and suddenly he saw his arm float into the next room. He kept saying that something was happening, but I didn't understand until I saw his mouth. He was talking, but the right side of his mouth wasn't moving. I realized that he was having a stroke. Then his arm became numb, and a shock ran through his wrist and elbow. I dialed 911 and helped him to the couch. I ran out to get on the mule, and it wouldn't move, so I ran down the hill to get Rod. I have since learned that I stripped the gears out of the mule. Oh well. Rodney said when he looked out his door and saw me running; he began to pray because he knew it was Dad. The next day he told me that if I had been carrying a football toward the end zone, no one could have kept me from scoring a touchdown. The grandkids still can't envision Mamaw running--period. At Jewish Hospital they went down through his throat and looked at his heart to discover a hole. The FDA will not allow doctors to close the hole until they have tried the coumadin.

October 7th, 2009

I spent the night in the waiting area with Paulette, Agnes, and a very loud Pepsi machine. About 9:30, I made myself a little nest in a corner behind the machine. I opened my computer to try to find the net. As I settled in for what I thought would be a very uncomfortable night, a lady peered around the corner and smiled. She wanted to know if I were staying all night. I really didn't want to be bothered. The day had been too long and scary for me, and I just wanted peace and quiet. She then informed me that she and her sister had squatting rights to that waiting area and that I must listen to their house rules. Suddenly, another lady bounced around the corner and introduced herself as Agnes, Paulette's sis. Ok, one was bigger than I and the other now meant two against one. I couldn't stay in Tommy's room, all the motels were full, and now, I thought, two black ladies were going to make this old fluffy white woman toe the mark in my last refuge. I guess they both realized, at the same time, that I was not completely in control of my emotions. Each gave me a hug and welcomed me aboard. I hope they didn't hear my relieved sigh. I became their "sugar" and "honey" for the rest of the night. They became my Angels of distraction. Instead of sleeping on chairs as I had planned, Tommy's nurse found me a cot. Paulette, Agnes, and I shared our lives, childhood memories, hopes and prayers for our sick, and laughed with energy until late. Their corner nest had food, clothes, bedding, and many other comforts of home. We finally tired and decided to sleep. I slipped off my shoes and snuggled down behind the Pepsi machine. I detected a pleasant, soothing aroma and leaned up to peek at the girls. They were applying face cream and putting spit curls in place with little metal hair clips. Paulette warned Agnes about her snoring and talking in her sleep. Agnes swore that she was not the one who was raucous at night. They both decided that I would be blamed for any night sounds. Sleep came quickly for me. Did you know that a 20 oz bottle of Pepsi bounces from side to side about eight times before it is jet propelled to the bottom to be retrieved by the customer who has just deposited $1.40 in small change. The only light in the area was the subtle glow of the machine. In my exhausted sleep, I did not recognize the sounds of the change slipping into the machine, as the Pepsi bounced its way through the chute, my inner alarm kicked in, but when the bottle reached its destination, I rose from the cot and peered around the machine. I didn't have time to fear for my safety, because the person leaning down to pick up his pop caught a glimpse of my shadow and immediately disappeared. I went back to my sleeping. I didn't think until the next morning whether the person actually grabbed his pop or just ran empty handed. Of course, I checked, and there was no Pepsi. Bless his/her heart; I hope he/she was able to enjoy that drink.

October 8th, 2009

Tommy doing fine on heparin and Coumadin. They found us a private room across the hall. So much better. I didn't want folks bringing in clothes so I just washed my clothes in the sink and put on scrubs. I went to breakfast this morning at the cafeteria. I remember when we had a Morrison's café in Owensboro. They have great food. I am not a breakfast person, but I can't resist walking through and looking over the great offerings. The hash browns looked luscious so I scooped some into my plate, then came the bacon. I checked the price and it was .49 for each piece. I passed the bacon. A young man stood beside me. He loaded his plate with bacon, and I began to worry that he didn't know the price. I said, ".49 is really expensive for bacon." He said, "sure is." I just took my potatoes and a biscuit to the checkout. He was checking out in front of me. The plate that had been full of bacon just held potatoes and bread. I watched as he paid and proceeded to a table. He sat behind a partition where he was fairly hidden. I sat behind him. And as any good detective does, I found a newspaper and peeked at him. Sure enough, he looked around and then reached into his jacket pocket to extract the hand full of bacon. He ate his meal and took out his wallet, went back through the line and did the same thing again. I have no comment. I feel sorry for anyone who is hungry. But, I don't know his circumstances.

October 9th, 2009

Today we are waiting for the Coumadin to reach therapeutic level. Then we will go to Rodney's for a few days. The doctors want us to stay in KY for a few weeks in case he has another episode. If he does, they will go in and patch the hole in his heart. We also need to check with his cardiologist in FL to see if they are adept in performing the type of surgery that they use here in Louisville. The surgeons here use the less invasive method to close the hole. Some doctors are not trained in this procedure and instead still use the open heart method. I have not left the hospital. They finally put us in matching scrubs, his are trimmed in yellow and mine are trimmed in pink. We are both doing fine today. Thanks for all your concern and prayers. God placed all of you in our pathway, and we were so wise to take you with us.

October 10th, 2009

Still in hospital, still thankful. We will probably leave here Monday. Tommy's main doctor wears cowboy boots and has a gun holster to carry his cell phone. No joke. He saw me as I wrote my emails and he wanted me to come to the doctors' station so he could show me a new program he uses for his patients. There I stood at the doc's station in my scrubs. I felt so important that I considered asking for a chart to update. I'm ok. I have been going over the scenarios of the last few weeks, and I am in awe of how signs in our lives are so plain to us in retrospect. Our kids and grands are glad that we are able to travel and spend time in FL. But this year they have all been anxious about our leaving. We both noticed this. We were planning to leave Oct. 5th, but we had to wait for some new tires for our truck to arrive. Our next date was set for Oct 12th. Then the stroke hit Oct 7th. If we had left on the 5th, Tommy would probably have been under the wheel. Maybe I am thinking too much in the abstract. I feel that when we finally head south, we will do so as a thankful couple.

Across Canada
June 15th, 2010

Good morning fellow travelers. I have wondered lately if we can expect anything to top our Alaska trip last year. So as usual, I just mulled it over for a few minutes and remembered that every day is ours, presented to us as a gift from God, and our actions and reactions belong to us. My first reaction came yesterday to one of Tommy's actions. He had spent lots of time inspecting my loading and storing methods inside the RV. He casually mentioned that he had no room left in "his" underbelly storage. Then he said he thought his guitar would fit beside the bed where I stored my banjo... that is with the banjo gone. I know, I have not played my instrument for two years, but the urge could overcome me anytime! Later, Lauren came across the yard carrying my banjo to store in Tom Jr.'s home. My reaction= being the calm, tolerant person that I am, I said nothing. As we pulled out of the drive to begin our trip he again casually mentioned that he may have to put his guitar in a closet. My new reaction= "what did you say?" He had stumped his toe on the end of the case, and he was afraid it may have to be moved. Excuse me; it is on his side of the bed. My short, fluffy toes will not be tramping there, so he will leave that guitar as is so that each blue toe reminds him how neatly my banjo fit into that spot. Staying at a nice park on Lake Shafer near his sister, Dar, in Indiana. Stormed badly. You haven't lived until you sit in a tin box with numerous windows and watch the lightening illuminate the inside as the rain and wind shake you around. Thank goodness it was supper time, and I was hungry and busy eating. I haven't checked the tents around us yet. But it was rough. Visit and lunch with family today, then off to WI. tomorrow for two days. Love ya.

June 16th, 2010

A beautiful day on Lake Shafer today. Tommy's sis, Dar, and brother-in-law, Louis, took us to a great place for lunch. Tommy had steak, ribs, potatoes, green beans, salad and ice cream for $10.00. Canadian geese having a ball in a neighbor's yard. He shoots at them with a pellet gun. They call him the goose man. The corn and bean fields are so green and neat. We did have some flooding last night, but all the tent people looked unscathed this morning. Just been checking out places to stay in Canada. The first thing I noticed were the cautions about the bears and moose. Lordy, here we go again. But I'm an old trooper at beast watching after last year. Leaving early morn to camp at Wisconsin Rapids with friends who are Florida snowbirds too. Tommy bought two new shirts today. Yep. Then he asked me how I had spent $70.00 at Wal-Mart. Let's see-- food, trash can, fly swatter, velcro, two shirts. Now you guess the items which cost the most! But, I would hate for him to run out of shirts and have to appear in public and expose his three grey chest hairs. Love you. bye from Lake Shafer, IN.

June 17th, 2010

Had a few travelers' woes today. Tail light on RV burned out, terrible traffic jam had to by-pass at Madison, WI, and Tommy left the steps out on the RV. All of these calamities were easily remedied. Campground store had the bulb, I routed us around the congestion, and my ever astute eyes caught view of the steps as we were pulling out of the rest stop. (I did leave the fridge door open, but that was minor, yep.) What a beautiful, bountiful, country we live in! The patches of wild flowers along the back roads were of every color, shape and size. I wanted to stop and fill my trailer with just a few of each one. Silly. I love all pretty plants, even if they are called weeds. A few weeks ago, I helped our grands pick wild flowers for their Mom. We decided to look up each name on the computer. Ty found one that said it was used to poison Romans. We hurriedly picked through the bunch we had in the sink to throw away what we thought were poison hemlock. Later that week we actually saw the same flowers for sale at Wal-mart= yarrow plants. Have arrived in Nekoosa, WI. We have no TV and very little phone reception. So if we need to know something please email soon. When in Alaska, we had no TV for weeks. Started receiving calls that we had had an earthquake in Anchorage, the Chinese had missiles pointed our way, Sarah Palin had resigned, etc. So just let us know if we are in peril. Our snowbird friends took us to a grand supper. We sat outside and reminisced then retired happy, full, and thankful. Good Night from Nekoosa, WI.

June 18th, 2010

I just looked at my log dates and found I had put the wrong date on the first one. We left home on the 15th of June. Lordy, I just wonder about me. Dan and Lee were set up at the Deer Trail Park when we arrived yesterday. They are such wonderful hosts. Today, after a great breakfast, in Saratoga, WI, they took us on a tour. My favorite was a cheese factory. I ate so many curds that I felt, as Lee says, like Little Miss Muffet. Am mailing some home for the kids. We saw our first cranberry bogs and learned how they are grown and harvested. Lots of potato crops here, so green and clean. We visited their beautiful home in Wisconsin Rapids and are waiting now for our supper to cook. Fresh green beans, grilled potatoes, salad and pork loin. Love all of you folks. God bless from Nekoosa, WI.

June 19th, 2010

It doesn't seem like Saturday. Dad died when I was twenty. That was my first realization that death was real and it hurt so different than any pain I had ever experienced. Fathers' day is a day to remember Dad, but I wish I could just give him a hug. Happy Fathers' Day to all you Daddies. We traveled through northern Wisconsin most of the day. The dairy farms are so neat. Sad to see some had shut down because of the economy. Deer are abundant here, also. We tried to identify the gorgeous tall flowers along the road and in some fields. They are wild Hyacinth. Trying to stay on the back roads, but a little scary because of the deer. Washed clothes in the sink tonight. We will be in Winnipeg tomorrow so I can do more laundry. Had to boil a dozen eggs tonight. I forgot that we can only take two dozen across the border. We cannot eat a dozen eggs tonight, so if they want any eggs they can have them. Can only take in tropical fruit. Have two bananas. Yep! Drove the shoreline of Lake Superior, then crossed it into Minnesota. Saw a huge bear drinking from a lake. I hate that Tommy can't see some things because he is driving. He will allow me to drive for only a few miles while he naps. But that is a man thing! In the 60's most of the day, a little cool. I think our money is worth a little more than Canadian, but if I have to use money instead of a card, they could give me Monopoly money and I wouldn't know the difference. Hard to find a campground for tonight because of Fathers' Day weekend. We are sitting on a hill above Pelican Lake, MN where they say the bluegills are the largest in the world. Saw a man come up the hill with some big ones, but all we have with us are ocean rods. I don't think the bluegills are that huge. Miss everyone. Will not be calling much for a few days and anyone who calls us while in Canada will be charged 79 cents a minute. Don't know what is in the news-still no TV. Love to ya and good night from Orr, Minnesota.

June 20th, 2010

Well, today was an eventful, funny, costly day. Awakened about 3:30 a.m. freezing. Tommy turned on the furnace about 7 and I was glad. As I was going to the bathroom, I forgot that there is an 8 inch step from the bed floor to the bathroom floor. When my old body hit the wall, it awakened sleeping beauty. Instead of saying, "Darling, what happened. Are you ok?" He yells, " What the hell are you doing? Don't you know that step is there by now?" Now, that's true love. Tommy bought propane just before we crossed the border----the first time. He was charged $73.00 for a tank that held only 2 gallon because they charge by the tank. I almost fainted. Our adventures were just beginning. The toll was $10.00 to cross the river to the border. Made it across the border fine. Lots of questions, but no problems. After traveling about 80 miles headed toward Winnipeg, we discovered that the road we were on would end in the lake. So our only recourse was to go back across the border into Minnesota and drive 36 miles then cross back into Canada at Manitoba. I am the navigator, so I was responsible. I didn't tell Tommy that you cannot cross into the U.S. with meat and some fruits in your possession. I knew he would freak out. I just prayed he would not see the big sign stating to declare all meat, fruit, and veggies. He missed the sign. I told him to not talk to customs. So I just explained to the man about our problem and he looked inside the trailer and let us through--meat, veggies, and bananas. After we arrived back in U.S., I told him about the law. So when we return at Vancouver we will need to have our ducks in a row. Fourth time may not be charm.

Then after 36 miles in MN, we started our trip back across the river. The lady asked a few questions and I explained again what "I" had done. She laughed and sent us on our way. Tommy bought a small bottle of Pepsi for $2.05. I wonder if the people in Canada are generous to old couples who have to stand on the street with a tin cup?

We have been to Windsor before, but never this far inland in CA. When I looked at the Manitoba map, I told Tommy we would be in towns and probably traffic most of the way to Winnipeg. We have been so amazed at the lack of people and traffic. We are staying only a few miles from Winnipeg and the huge, and I mean huge, farms are still all around us. The owners of this park are so friendly. Hamburgers for supper (made with ground beef that has made three border crossings) We still have no TV. Well, we have one channel tonight and it is iffy, so please catch me up on any important news. Going sightseeing tomorrow, then on to Saskatchewan Tuesday. (I have to look up the spelling of that word every time I use it.) Until tomorrow, from us to you all with love from Ile-des-Chenes, Canada.

June 21st, 2010

Rained all day. Slept late. Great to just lie in bed in a trailer and doze off again and again. Did laundry at the RV park. A young man came in while I was waiting for my clothes to dry. I needed to help him use the washer. He called me "Miss" That was nice. To Walmart in Winnipeg. Small store. High prices. We have tried to keep up with the prices which are listed in dollars, then the difference shows up at the bank. The money must be close to Canadian value because we see a very small difference when it is deducted from our account. Gas is, of course, sold by liters. We have a converter on our GPS. It helps but still is confusing for us. When we crossed the border(the first time), the speed limit read 90. There is also a km on the truck, so we were able to figure the speed from it. It is still odd to look up and see maximum speed as 100. I have learned 5 French words. Est, Sud, Nord, Ouest, and sortie. I also learned that I must read all the rules of the campgrounds here. Early this week, I found a beautiful campground and at a reasonable price. While searching through the rules of the campground, my eyes caught a sentence. Clothes are optional. OOps! I told Tommy and he immediately wanted to know the location. I try to not even envision a scenario of us driving into a nudist campground. But, you can be sure that I check all the rules closely now before making any reservations. Lazy, peaceful day today. Headed for Regina, SK tomorrow. Love you all from far away Winnipeg, Manitoba.

June 22nd, 2010

Left for SK early this morn. We have discovered that 100 km equal 62.1 miles so the mileage from place to place here is in Km. Thank you GPS. It converts to miles. I drove some today. Just as I turned onto the highway, the sky dumped. I felt like Chicken Little for awhile. We ate our usual snacks for lunch. I prepare a little picnic on the console and we nibble away. Still eating that great WI cheese. I had planned to send some home to the kids, but Tommy is so eating it every day. It is not binding like I have always heard that cheese is usually. I guess that was a little too much information. Yep! Hit my right arm on a cabinet door, made a nice blue spot, still have a blue mark from falling out of the bedroom, and Tommy still has no blue toes. I guess that is called karma. We are in Indian Head, SK for two nights at KOA campground. As I was checking in, the nice gentleman gave me papers to show the local attractions. While I was perusing the papers, he asked me if we were headed west through Regina. My face turned red and I said, "Pardon me." He asked me again if we were headed through Regina. Trying not to laugh, I told him yes. Folks this ole Kentuckian pronounces Regina as a girlfriend's name I knew in school, and as a friend of Mom's years ago. Here Regina rhymes with a personal part of a lady's anatomy. That is as far as I will take this. I hope when we go into town tomorrow, that I do not ever need to use the name. Oh, guess which campground is 15 minutes from us. It sits in a beautiful valley with pure blue lakes and green, green, grass. We are going to tour the town tomorrow, but that will be the extent of our participation. I'm getting ready to eat supper, then plan us to Washington State. We already have reservations to stay in Bellingham WA for 4 nights, 2,3,4,5 of July. Now after Calgary, we must climb the Canadian Rockies, then spend time in Vancouver. So we will be back in the states July 2. We have had no TV. Well, we found one channel for two days.. I know why I see so many slim Canadians. Also, I have never seen so much farm land ever. Cows, cows and more cows. Beautiful. Talk again tomorrow from Indian Head, Saskatchewan (learned to spell it now without help).

June 23rd, 2010

What a sweet day. Rained early, the sun stayed with us the rest of the day. I am including three pictures. One is of a church on a little hill. Another is Tommy and I with an Indian. One is poor Tommy trying to de-mud my expensive $14.00 Beals sandals. That is what happens when you take the back roads. But, we love the scenery better than cities. I know that I have seen farm country all over the U.S., but these are some of the largest I have seen. Many are planted, but some have flooded. We toured the tiny old town of Indian Head--thus the photo. Then we traveled through a beautiful valley called Qu Appelle. Somewhere hidden away in that valley is the nudist campground. I have never seen so many gravel and dirt roads, not even in Alaska. These folks have so much room and space even in the towns. It may be different when we get to Vancouver, but so far the only traffic jam we have been in has been construction. We headed to Wal-mart in Regina, but stopped across the road to get gas. A nice, handsome gentleman told us that the store across from Wal-mart would give us cash back for gas bought. As Tommy filled our tank, a man came out of the station. He hit a container, which contained paper towels to clean the windshield, popped it open a took every towel and put them in his truck. He looked to be about 70 years old. Should be ashamed. I shopped in my first true Canadian store. I had a ball. There were so many odd foods and I tried to read all the labels in French until a lady told me to turn the cans, etc , around and I would find English on most things. I know another French word, "vert." Our groceries were $80.81, but with the gas discount and coupons I had, it was $66.14. Nice! I thought we would never find a cart. Tommy finally figured out that we had to put a dollar in the handle to get a cart, then when we returned it our money would come back to us. There were no carts sitting in that parking lot. First we couldn't find a place to put the money. Then we figured out that you had to have a Canadian dollar coin. Tommy just bought a man's cart as he finished with it and gave him an American dollar. As we were going to the truck, a lady wanted to buy our cart. She gave us a Canadian coin and we gave her a U.S. dollar. Tommy tried to buy himself a Pepsi, but his money would not work. A lady saw him and gave him the correct money for American money. We arrived back at the park to discover that there had been a quake in Ontario and the road we needed to cross tomorrow to Calgary is washed out. I had nothing to do with either. God's love to all. We miss everyone so much. Talk to you from Calgary tomorrow. Good Night from Indian Head, SK.

June 24th, 2010

Long, long drive today. Stormed again this morn. Canada is drowning. I'm so glad we have a 4x4. The main road to Calgary was washed away in one small area, but there are so few paved roads in this area that we had to detour 160 miles. I know you have heard this before , but they have the fattest cows I have ever seen. Gophers are all over. They are so cute. They stand on the side of the road and try to skitter across safely. Sometimes I root for them by yelling, " Hurry, hurry, or wait ,wait!" Tommy finally flattened one today. He said, " Oops, I got one." I'm glad I didn't see it. I have decided that if I ever get rich, I want to be a landlocked Noah. I want to fence in 100 acres, build a home in the middle and have hundreds of sweet animals running free so I can watch them, feed them and love on them. I would need to closely supervise Tommy Sr. and Pam, Rod's wife, they have been rough on the dog and cat population. We arrived at a park near Calgary tonight. It is dry, very clean and sits on Bow River at the foothills of the Canadian Rockies. There is plenty of snow up high and cool enough for heat here. Wish I could send some down south. Everyone be careful, please. Don't stay out for long. Guess I will do some laundry tomorrow. We try to wear our clothes more than one day since I don't have a washer in this unit. My boys were freaked out that we use our towels twice. They should have had to take a bath in the same water as two other people had already bathed in. That was our Saturday or Sunday bath routine until I was eleven years old. Everyone here has been so friendly and helpful. Well, one young woman almost had to eat ditch weeds when she passed me in her little red car as I and other vehicles were trying to move to the left lane to avoid a semi which had wrecked and was burning on the side of the road. Made me angry so I blew Tommy's loud funny horns and almost scared her out of her scarf. Yep! I'm ok. I'm not sure about Tommy. Scared that man. Try to say cool. More love your way tomorrow from Calgary, Alberta, CA.

June 25th, 2010

It still seems odd to put a date like 2010 on anything. I wrote 19-- for 55 years, then the century had to change on me. Well, we had a few scary moments for a little while this morn. Neither of us knew the correct time. Domafatcher (Tommy) has been putting all the clocks on different times. I tuned in to wifi and I had not set it for daylight savings, so then we were really bummed. Since our phones did not change, we were again confused, until I figured out that Manitoba and Saskatchewan are in the same time zone. Most of you know that my husband is addicted to diet Pepsi. We bought a case today and discovered that we must pay $2.40 deposit for a case because each can is worth 10 cents in CA. I think I will backtrack and retrieve his cans so we can pay for the rest of our trip. I hate to let the sons hear this, but we stopped in an old school yard park to refresh ourselves. While I was fixing a sandwich, Tommy took a ride on a merry-go-round. He didn't tell me until after the fact. It's a good thing his ride was successful because he would still be lying there? If I don't get to a TV soon, I am going to need some settle down pills. I miss Bill, Glenn, and Sean. I miss Drew, too. We should have TV by 28th. And I will not watch Cops when we do! Well, he can watch it while I read or write. Although we enjoyed the agriculture regions of Canada, we are really looking forward to the Rockies. I have noticed in the literature that there seems to be more towns developed in these mountains than U.S. I don't know if that is good or bad. But we are excited. Just came back from a walk by the river. Three wet dogs passed us and headed back to the water. When they emerged, soaked, guess who got wet. What does a wet dog do to dry? The owner apologized with a smile on his face and hurried along. Tommy was not smiling nor was he spouting nice words. I'm glad he didn't look at me. I know he had planned to wear those clothes a few more days.

Pot of beans for supper. Hot peppers and salad plate with cukes, tomatoes, carrots, and green onions.

Good Night from Calgary, AB.

June 26th, 2010

Pretty today. Rained last night. Made it over the Canadian Rockies. Staying at the foothills of Canadian Glacier Park. So funny, the guy who checked us into this park used to live in Ft Myers, FL. I have a gift for all of you. I am hoping this will help cool you down some. If Tommy says one more word about how dirty the truck and RV are, I think I will scream. We have been in mud and dust and gravel so much that there is no reason to clean these vehicles. When we cross Montana and Wyoming it will be just as dusty. Only saw a few elk in the mountains. Stopped at Lake Louise in the top of the rockies and took a lift to the top of a mountain--very nice. Here is a little funny. When our boys were growing up, they would not drink Dollar Store chocolate milk mix. They wanted Nestles Quick only. We bought a huge can of Nestles. When it was empty, we filled it with Dollar Store brand. They drank it, I guess, until they left for college. When the can became worn, we had to replace it. but they never knew the difference. Now, here is what reminded me of this story. We went shopping at this great Canadian store. They had lots of coupons and lots of, what they labeled "no name" products. I bought Tommy some "no name" Cherrios. The next day as we were traveling along, he suddenly said, " You really get what you pay for, don't you." I didn't know what he was speaking about, but he continued by saying that his cereal was not as good as his real Cherrios. I laughed so hard. I had not even opened the new box of cereal. Now tell me---like father like sons! I'm glad Tommy doesn't like to write or want to proofread my emails. He may want to tell some stories on me. Can't imagine what! We love everyone and miss everyone. I learned two new French words today--fin and arret. I figure at this pace I should be fluent in the language by the time I am 102 years old. As we were going through Safeway yesterday, I noticed this little fellow who was not happy sitting in a shopping wagon being pushed by his Mom. She stopped beside me to pick up some jelly. With arms crossed, a scowl on his cute little face, and in the Canadian accent I have learned to love, he looked at his Mom and said, "How much longer are we shopping? You are really ruining my day." I had to hurry along as I laughed. He must have been only 3 yrs old. Kids, I love them, and then I take them back home. We have cable tonight! There is a catch. All the news is Canadian with a bit of U.S. Imagine that. I love some of the commercials up here. Good Night from Revelstoke, BC.

June 27th, 2010

We had a lazy day. Rained some. I read and wrote and ate and cried and laughed . I watched a big turtle for about an hour and he never moved. Finally, an RV moved in that space. The folks just walked around the turtle and walked away. They didn't like the site and moved out. My nosy got to me. I walked over and discovered the largest mushroom I have ever seen. It never moved. Viewed a damn at the Columbia River; Tommy's legs hurt so badly that he said he probably would not drive us through Glacier. We will hire a guide, I guess, because he won't ride through with me. He loves to ride the Ski lifts. They hurt my legs. If you all hear that we are on a Canadian Wanted list, it is because I think we entered the parks without paying. As we entered, there were 5 lanes, and one that said something about free access. Of course, we hit that lane and kept on trucking. Suddenly, a police car appeared from the other lane. We both let out a sigh of relief when the police pulled over another truck. Someone said they have cameras that take pictures, so we may receive a notice from the RCMP. We're ok. Yep! Revelstoke, BC.

June 28th, 2010

I know we have America the Beautiful, now I can say Canada the Beautiful. Today was our most wonderful drive so far. There were beautiful meadows full of red, yellow, and white flowers, trees, mountains. We saw a large chocolate colored moose with her red/brown calf drinking from a clear, blue lake. After stopping at the RV park in Vancouver, BC, we did not like it so we decided to continue on to Washington State. We will be here until July 6, because the other parks are filled for the Fourth of July. Most people are off Monday for that holiday. Then staying one night in far east WA. At Columbia Falls, Montana for Tommy's July 9th birthday. I have the U.S. cable TV. Am I happy, well I should say. I don't live in front of the thing, but I must keep up with this ole USA. I know Canadians are glad I have left ; they had two earthquakes, a terrible tornado, riots in Toronto, and damaging floods. Oh heavens, a plane just about came through the RV. We are just a short distance from the international airport, and Tommy just came in to tell me to watch the ravens. He was attacked while taking a walk. These birds are as large as our turkey birds. So now all I need is a nice set of ear plugs and a large tough umbrella. Having music here for the 4th. Speaking of music, the Canadians play lots of country and bluegrass. I admire them for their concern for the environment. They seriously recycle. I read a sign today that said the 7 million dollars used for a road came from recycling money. Most people that I saw shopping had their own carry-out bags. Kudos to Canadians. Have so much to do here. Don't know what to do first. We are on the Pacific and a few miles from the Cascades and short time to Victoria. Loving all of you from Bellingham, WA.

June 29th, 2010

Laundry day! Lordy, had three loads this time. Tommy does all the moving from washer to dryer and helps fold. I just sit and read my Kindle until all is ready. Poor Tommy and his wisps of white hair flying about have attracted this momma bird. When he told me about the bird attacks earlier, I thought it was one of these big ravens that will run toward you if they think you have food. I pictured Edgar Allen Poe's raven "knock, knock, knocking" on his head. But, when we went to the laundry, this cute little black bird popped him again. Yes, it is not a raven, just a small black local breed of some kind. His last trip out, he took a paper with him and scared the poor thing badly. Maybe this drama is over. We drove to the bay yesterday to admire the many sail boats and fishing boats. Also, went to Wal-Mart. I think we have the best Wal-Marts I have ever visited right there in KY. Some folks do not like that store, but I have found that most of anything I need, I find it there and cheaper. Meatloaf and mac & cheese for supper. Able to talk to all my babies now that we are out of CA. If one called us there, it cost 79 cents a minute. Yep! I am so glad that Tommy and I agree it is ok to just rest for some days. Tomorrow we are going sightseeing. We have a screw in one tire and have knocked the front end out of line, so off to the garage too. Love ya, from WA.

June 30th, 2010

My goodness, we slept until 9 a.m.. Noticed the first major storm was named after our youngest grandson, Alex. Humm! He is actually a sweet, rotten, smart, loveable, 8-year-old. Toured Bellingham, took the truck to a tire fix-it place, shopped at one of my favorite stores, picked up a part for rv , and arrived home tired. Good news at the tire place. They took out the screw that left no leak and told us we did not need a front alignment. Spotted a vegetable market and had to stop. We were really headed to a farmers' market down by the bay. However, the prices were great so we purchased WA sweet onions, green onions, cukes, and tomatoes. I wanted to wait to buy some products at the other market. Well, what a pretty market they had at the bay, but again I had one of my almost fainting spells when we saw the prices. Examples: tomatoes $5.00 lb., strawberries $5.00 a pint, green onions $3.00 a bunch (we had just bought some for 39 cents a bunch). There were people actually buying things! We then headed to Whatcom Falls Park which should have been only a few miles away. I received a phone call and Domafatcher missed our turn. Ten minutes later he said there is a sign that says Sudden Valley 10 miles ahead. I told him we were not going to a valley; we were going to a waterfall. We ended at Sudden Valley. It was a very pretty drive. We stopped and bought some picnic supplies and headed back to our original destination. The falls was worth the trip. Then went shopping at Fred Myers. We had shopped at one in Alaska. I love the store. It has Kroger products but is about four times larger and many other departments. Planning a train trip to

Vancouver tomorrow. Night All Love to ya.

July 1st, 2010

Today is my sweet Aunt Zeula's birthday. We lost her in 1996. She left us with many precious memories. I awakened this morning with gout in my right ankle. For anyone who has ever had gout, you know how I felt. I took my first pill at 4:30 a.m. My pills are old so I called my doc in FL and she is calling in more meds. The train trip is off for tomorrow, but I should be able to move about some. Tommy got so tired of being inside that he washed the rv windows. Wish he had vacuumed and mopped and dusted the inside. I forgot to tell you all what was for sale at the high-priced farmers market at the bay. Now, I won't say anything explicit, but they were called Amy's Washable Monthly Rags. When I first saw her booth, I didn't read her sign. I thought she was selling eye-glasses holders, but couldn't figure out why there were so many shapes and sizes. Of course, nothing escapes Tommy. He looked at me and I just told him not to ask until later. The park is filling up for the 4th holiday. The park owners are grilling on Sunday, and we are taking a dish to pass. A band will be playing country and bluegrass. No dancing for me. Everyone is taking a canned item for the local food bank. I think I will make breaded tomatoes. Called Rod today to see if they would allow our 16 -year-old grandson to fly out and ride home with us since his baseball season is over. What a treat that would be for us. I stayed in my gown all day. I am feeling better tonight. Hope all is well for everyone. Love and hugs from us. WA.

June 27th, 2010

We had a lazy day. Rained some. I read and wrote and ate and cried and laughed . I watched a big turtle for about an hour and he never moved. Finally, an rv moved in that space. The folks just walked around the turtle and walked away. They didn't like the site and moved out. My nosy got to me. I walked over and discovered the largest mushroom I have ever seen. It never moved. Viewed a damn at the Columbia River; Tommy's legs hurt so badly that he said he probably would not drive us through Glacier. We will hire a guide, I guess, because he won't ride through with me. He loves to ride the Ski lifts. They hurt my legs. If you all hear that we are on a Canadian Wanted list, it is because I think we entered the parks without paying. As we entered, there were 5 lanes, and one that said something about free access. Of course, we hit that lane and kept on trucking. Suddenly, a police car appeared from the other lane. We both let out a sigh of relief when the police pulled over another truck. Someone said they have cameras that take pictures, so we may receive a notice from the RCMP. We're ok. Yep! Revelstoke, BC.

July 2nd, 2010

Thank the sweet Lord, my ankle is better. We ventured out for a short drive to a local Indian Nation called Lummi Nation. It borders the Georgia Straits of the Pacific. Finally able to pick up my meds at the pharmacy now that my foot is better. They had my name wrong. Florida had sent the script in my middle name. I think I will save the med pack in case I have another flare up. I listed our truck and RV on Ebay today. Tommy was determined to keep the truck, but with much discussion and logic, he gave in. We will be looking for a cheap van to take to Florida and leave so we can fly back and forth. Then we will purchase a C Class for our summer vacations. We have enjoyed the RV on this trip, and I love the floor plan. We just don't need this much room for short trips. Still have Glacier Park, which we have never seen, then to Cat Creek, Montana for some business, then to Yellowstone. We have not been to Yellowstone since the 80's so I know we will love it again and have more time to enjoy the numerous wildlife. Going from there to visit good friends we met while playing music in FL. Watch out Ed and Pat, here we come. I always warn people to never say "come to see us" because now that we have an RV, they could find us parked in their yard anytime I really enjoy sharing our days with you folks; I just worry sometime that someone is saying "Lordy, here she is again." Please feel free to do as you please with this stuff. Just don't tell me because I promise I will get revenge. Yep! We love all of you(even Paul), remember he is our adopted son from FL. Unless he acts up and displeases me, then I un-adopt him for awhile. Tommy is fussing because the floor is dirty. Guess time to vacuum. He is so darn old and finicky. Love all of you. Miss all of you. Cool down that weather and we will be home in late July.

July 3rd, 2010

Cool again last night. Yesterday, I thought we were settled in for the night when Tommy decided he wanted me to find a Jack in the Box so he could have a milkshake. At 9 p.m. we were in downtown ordering a chocolate shake. Then he wanted to go to Meyers for hot pepper for his beans. I did not feel like walking so I got in a scooter. The scooter wouldn't back up so I tried to see if it was out of juice. As I pushed on reverse, the scooter in front of mine started moving. After a few choice mummerings, I just decided I would try to walk. Then I noticed that I was hooked to the arm of the front scooter. I finally disengaged the two buggies and hit reverse. I heard a man say something like "watch out" as I whizzed past his leg. Lordy, where was Domafatcher all this time? Potty? When I have to use a scooter, I feel like everyone is looking for my disability. I tried to prop up my swollen ankle so they could see it. We had been discussing what I would take to our cookout tomorrow when Tommy saw these guys setting up music amps, etc. It seems the cookout was today, not tomorrow. I hurriedly fixed, what I call baked chili. The band did a great job. Some gentleman showed up who played keyboard as a profession. Wow, is all I can say. Tommy is going to ask him tomorrow to see if he wants to jam some. I wanted to pat my sore foot to the wonderful music, but I just clapped my hands and enjoyed. I am going to try to send a small video clip. The key word here is "try." I have been asked to go back to Jack in the Box tonight. Nope. He had cherry pie for dessert at the party. I have an unspoken prayer request. Just send up some extra words for someone special in our lives. Appreciate it. Thanks for listening again. We love you all. We love the freedom to express our love for God.

July 4th, 2010

When young, I took freedom for granted. Now, since I have shed some of my youth and ignorance, I bow down to our awesome military. Yes, today I celebrate our independence, but I can never find the profound combination of words to thank all those people who love their America and its citizens enough to risk and give the ultimate: their lives. Thank you. I love you. We climbed Mt. Baker today. Now, don't get an image of two old farts easing their way from rock to rock to limb as we start an ascent of some 6,000 feet. We rode a Ford. So much beauty on this earth. We have worn our eyeballs out looking for bears, and I get word from home that a man was attacked by a bear in eastern KY. Tom Jr. said DNA results show that hair found in Marion County, KY is that of a bear. That is the county where Tommy and the boys have their hunting land. I have only been to the land once, but I may have to come home to see a bear. When in Florida, folks are told to zig-zag if you find the need to run from an alligator because they have to stop before they can turn. Then, here, and throughout the bear country we have been in, they tell folks to lie down and pretend to be dead. Yep! The key word for me in that incident would be "pretend." And if I ever have to run from an alligator, he could never catch me unless he had deep traction tires to get through the substance I would be leaving behind. Tommy played in the snow. Parts of the roads were blocked by 3 feet of snow and ice. Lakes were still covered in ice. Too cold for me. I stayed in the truck except to take a few pics. As soon as we arrived home, I covered with an afghan and turned on the heater. Fireworks scheduled at 10 and domafatcher (someone told me I spelled this wrong) wanted to go. They were beautiful. We were lucky to get the vehicle close enough to watch from inside. He mentioned a milkshake, but he had eaten a huge container of butter pecan while in the mountains. Only he can find that stuff in no man's land. No milkshake. The fireworks were shot over the bay and did not start until 10:15 because it doesn't get real dark until about 11. Thanks for the prayers and back to all. Every night, I read until I, as Aunt Zeula used to say, begin blinking like a frog in a hailstorm, then I close my eyes and begin my talk with my Savior. Some nights the comfort of having Him there with me and to know He is listening puts me to sleep too quickly to share all my concerns. But He knows my thoughts even as I rest. Peace and love, coming to you tonight from us.

July 5th, 2010

Laundry day. Just two loads. Filled diesel tanks and found long lines to the pumps reminded us of old days of gas shortage. On to Wal-Mart for essentials-- Pepsi and paper towels. Been writing lots today. Truck hooked up. Will have to set the alarm because we have been staying in bed late. Tomorrow will be a long, beautiful mountain drive. We will probably make it home about the 22 or 23 of July. Saw a young lady who reminded me of my niece, Tammy. Cried. Tommy says someone will be 68 the 7th. I think it was the 2nd. Her initials are DD. . July is a big birthday month for us too. Tom Sr. 9th, Tom Jr. 14th, Lauren 22nd, Oliver 25th and Ty 26th. Warming up here so we need to get out. Easy day. Quiet day. Last night to say bye from Bellingham, Washington.

July 6th, 2010

On the road again! My eyeballs are tired again. If anyone ever heads west by the north route, stay off the interstate and take route 20 across the Cascades to the Pacific. It's all there: ocean, mountains, valleys of wild flowers, heather meadows, snow, waterfalls, creeks, lakes, rivers, purple sage, etc. Tommy is still looking for that bear. He thinks one should walk to the edge of the road and wave a white flag at us. I'm sure we will see them in Yellowstone, but he thinks that is not wild enough. The last time we stayed in Yellowstone, we were told to take no food to our cabins. Well, he took our bologna and cheese in our place and during a terrible storm, enjoyed our picnic. Then early morning we heard unusual noises near our door. At daylight, we peeked out and discovered that the big animals, moose and bear had come down to sniff at the doors and dump barrels. When I think of bears, I think of the time we took Tommy's Mom and Dad to the Smokie Mountains. I read until about 3 in the morn. I heard noises on the deck, but had no desire to look out. The next day we found muddy bear tracks across the porch. When we returned from supper that night, although I always let Mom hold my arm for support as we walked, I told her that when that car door opened, I was gone. She couldn't believe I would run and leave her, but when the door opened she actually beat me to the door. She was so sweet. We are parked near the FDR lake and dam. Will leave the RV hooked up since we are here for one night. When we got out of the trailer, we heard a loud mooing/grunting sound. I asked Tommy what that noise was. He told me it was a moose. We went to the edge of the hill behind us but saw nothing. Then he followed the sound. It was the neighbor's water faucet. Tommy picked me a beautiful wildflower. I am going on line to see what it is. I will include a few pics today. Hope you all enjoy them. Good Night from Kettle Falls, Washington.

July 7, 2010

Tommy says some old woman turns 68 today. I think it was the 2nd of July. His main point is that he won't be 68 until Friday. Sorry Wanda, he made me write this. I forgot to mention yesterday that we traveled through the orchards in WA. There were apples, peaches, bing cherries mainly. Lots of grapes too. I felt like a contestant on "Who Wants to be a Millionaire" who had polled the audience when I opened my email this morning. I think 99% of you folks knew the flower was a foxglove. I have seen them many times, but have never been close to one. Aren't they precious. Trish told me not to put it in food. She is a nurse and said something about medicine in them. Lordy, if I suddenly meet my demise, check to see what flowers Tommy has been picking for me. I have various weak points, one is identifying plants and trees. I do very well with fruit and nut trees if they are in the production stage, otherwise, I know mainly palm and weeping willow. As we were leaving Kettle Falls this morn, there right in the middle of a railroad track stood a gorgeous deep brown elk with his woman beside him. I told Tommy they were just calming waiting to cross the highway. He said he really thought they were waiting to catch a train. He tries! We are in a nice park in Columbia Falls, Montana at the foothills of Glacier Park. Planning to ride the park shuttle over the mountain. We finally had a lunch out today--McDonalds. I bought Tommy two double cheeseburgers, and he said he was full after the first one. I advised him to just take it with him for later. He decided to eat it because he was afraid it would not be there when he wanted it later.

Then he said something about our plane trip to Alaska. Yep! I'll remember that remark. Shopped in another huge store tonight. It was nice. Just called The Western Store. But it was all groceries and open 24hrs. Must get in the hay. Early morn for us. Love to all from Montana.

July 8th, 2010

What a smooth day...so far. They actually have free shuttles that will take folks across the Glacier. I'm so happy; Tommy finally was able to see the awesome sights in mountain trips. Our first time to take public transportation was years ago in D.C. We really enjoyed it even though we were the only people who could speak English except the guide. Then we hired a guide for Grand Canyon. We were so pleased to find the free shuttles here. Also, glad we did not wait until the weekend crowd. Our first ride was on a 31 ft bus which took us up about 7 miles. We then transferred to a smaller shuttle to go to the top. So neat what happened next. No one was waiting at the time this shuttle arrived, so we rode to the top with the driver and us. He was not supposed to, but he gave us a running narrative of the sights. Pretty, pretty, pretty! We had a small traffic jam as a large ram came down to join the tourists. I didn't pack food. I figured there would be, at least, snacks at the stops. I did not eat breakfast so, by 12, I was hungry. Next time I head out anyplace, I am stopping at McDonald's to fill my purse. We were able to find a nice restaurant at the bottom of the mountain. Tommy had a huge buffalo burger, diet Pepsi, and a huckleberry cobbler smothered in huckleberry ice cream. I had a great spinach veggie wrap. The bill was $28.00 , eight belonged to Ardoth. I did taste his dessert and "wow." He may replace some of those shakes for huckleberry "whatever." Everything you can imagine is made from hucks. It is fresh cherry, peach and huckleberry time here. Never had even seen one before. Went to Flathead River dam. Nice short drive. It is sad, but catches ones' eyes. There is a small white cross for those who have lost their lives on the Montana roadways. One place had five crosses in the same spot on the side of the road. May go to the National Bison Range tomorrow. Special hello, and a big ole hug to Scotty.

July 9th, 2010

Fifty years ago today, I bought Tommy a swim suit and matching shirt for his 18th birthday. We had been dating for about two months. Six months later we married. I was fifteen and he was eighteen. Now, we have been blessed with two great sons , six grandsons and one granddaughter. When I think of Rod having five boys, I remember when he was about ten years old, he became very angry with me because I would not allow him to drink a cola for breakfast. I still see him with those boney arms crossed, staring at me with disdain, and informing me that when he married, he would have ten kids and bring them all to my house and let them drink cola for breakfast. After number five, I began to worry. Tom Jr. had the boy and girl. I almost tore my kitchen apart when they showed me her sonogram and we found no male parts. When Rod was born he was supposed to be an eight pound girl named Cindy Carol. (C.C.) Well, we had to hurry to name our ten pound boy. Peyton Place was popular and I loved Rodney from the series. When Tom Jr. came along, we didn't have a girl name chosen because we wanted a boy so badly. We always knew that he would be our Junior. We talked with a couple while riding a shuttle. I thought the two children were their grands. The eight -year-old asked me where my kids were. After explaining that my kids were grown. I told them how young we were when we married. The Mom just stared at me in disbelief. She pondered a while and asked if that was the trend in my area. I bit my tongue. Then she wanted to know if my children got an education before marrying. I told her that they not only received their degrees, I was young enough to go to college with them. She pondered again. I waited! I then felt sorry for her. She expressed their concern as to whether they would even be around to see their children through college. Trip to Wal-mart today, truck wash, and nice steak supper for birthday boy. Sleeping late tomorrow. A deer ran in front of us, but we were driving slowly so no danger. Warming up here. In the eighties today. You all pray for our nephew Scotty. He is very ill. Love to all tonight. Talk tomorrow.

July 11th, 2010

"Home, Home on the Range, where the Deer and the Antelope Play." That's the song I have been singing today. We have had to let deer cross the road and have seen two herds of antelopes. Ok folks, I came from a small county of approximately 10,000 people. Today we visited Petroleum County, MT. The size is about 10 times my home county, with a population of about 600, yes, the whole county=600 folks. It has two cities. One is Winnit and actually the county court house is there. It is the 6th smallest in the US by population. Then we went to a place called Cat Creek which has three houses and some cows. Dirt and gravel roads and Tommy kept worrying about getting his truck dirty and being lost. What a hoot. We were amazed that there is so much land and so few people here. Staying in a town called Lewistown. Nice little place. Even has a McDonalds. Tina said someone reported seeing a Boa Constrictor come down a ditch and enter the pond where we stay in FL. No more fishing in the pond for Ardie. Love all. From Lewistown, MT.

July 12th, 2010

"Where Seldom is Heard a Discouraging Word and the Skies are not Cloudy all Day." Well, now folks, that first line of the range song is true, but let me tell you about this line. The discouraging words were from Domafatcher, who worried about all the dirt and mud on his truck again. I was having so much fun that I didn't care about the messy roads. Now I will address the non-cloudy day. That does not apply to the nights. Since I have only two TV channels and they have mostly silly shows, I seldom turn it on. Didn't have a weather report. As I lay my head on the pillow and picked up my Kindle, a gust of wind attacked the bedroom end of our RV. Then a clap of thunder actually shook the blinds, which, by the way, are supposed to be night shades--not so. The windows lit up as if someone had torched a bonfire. It didn't help that we have a skylight directly over our bed. I hunkered under the quilt. Tommy tried to reassure me that we would be fine and that the storm would be over soon. I wasn't as worried about the length of time, I was worried about lying somewhere outside bent, broken up and worst of all, half naked. He has not been able to comfort me much anyway since the time we were alone near Cedar Key and walking through the swamps. I spotted a huge track and asked him what he thought it might be. He assured me that it was a big dog track--not so. I didn't notice that he had picked up a large stick and was sharpening it with his knife. A panther track does not look like a dog track, but I didn't know that until we were safely back in the truck. However, the bright side to the storm was that it washed all the mud and dust from the truck. So off we go to see the Lewis and Clark National Forest and Crystal Lake. I found it on the map, but there were no signs leading us to it. While driving down the main road, he saw a sign that read, "Crystal Lake Road." I assured him that it was the road to the forest. Guess what? I'm just going to pause for a moment while you guess! The road was gravel. Yep! I am so glad we traveled the rough dusty road. It was like finding a quiet, uninhabited piece of paradise. The high road was scary but beautiful. When we reached the top, there were maybe eight people around the area. Great day. Now here is another guess. What is the first thing we did before we went to do laundry? Here are a few pics. One of the dirty truck. One of Crystal Lake, and a stream we followed all day. Hugs, love, kisses, peace to all. Cody, WY tomorrow.

July 13th, 2010
Made it to Cody. Did not need to travel on any gravel or dirt roads. Saw elk and antelope munching on ranchers crops. We couldn't identify many of the huge planted fields. Some looked like turnips. Arrived at our new campgrounds to discover that we have no TV. S***! I miss my news. Going to pack a picnic lunch and head to Yellowstone tomorrow. Then next day going to see wild horses and see our first live rodeo. We finally found a Wal-mart. Bought picnic supplies. Came home and gave Tommy a hair trim. Made him a bowl of pinto beans with hot peppers, green onions, fried side bacon for supper. Tommy bought an RV part and the lady who assisted him has relatives who live south of Owensboro. I don't know why people keep asking us if we are from the south. Cool last night. Had to turn on the heat for a while. Warm here in Cody. I was just mentally philosophizing about life today as we drove through the diverse, beautiful, natural sites provided for us free because we are free. I have seen the ruins of third world countries which at some time in our history were also, and a few still are, grand. But their inability to achieve the freedom we have has led to destruction of their lives and lands. I am one thankful lady every day for America. The more I explore, the more I love the land and the people. There are bitter folks everywhere, but they are outnumbered by the kind and caring. I know this, because I have been here 65 years. My little sis, Janice, keeps me grounded most of the time. When I become irritated by the assholes, she reminds me to be thankful for the kind people because most have found God. Then she

reminds me to pray for the others. Yep! That's my Jaybug. Dad gave her that name sixty years ago. Tomorrow is a special day. A child gave birth to a child. He will be 49 years old. Sleepy. Good night and thanks for listening.

July 14th, 2010

Today is so special in so many ways. I had better warn you folks. I am full of thankful emotions and thoughts that must come out before I retire for the night. The most important event took place 49 years ago, when I gave birth to our Tom Jr. McLean County Hospital was fairly new then. I screamed and screamed and screamed. In those days the father was not allowed to even visit the expectant mother in the labor room and heaven forbid he be allowed in the delivery room. It was probably a good thing I did not see him during my labor. Dr. Scott had to deliver him in his street clothes, because he arrived so late Tom's head had crowned. Some tall, large, older lady(about 30 years old) kept telling me to stop yelling. She told me that she had had two children and had never carried on like that. The pain was worth the gain. Tom is special and has presented us with our first grandchild and our only little girl grand. Men just don't understand. Do they ladies? When I become emotional, Tommy always wants to know what is wrong. Then try to explain and he still doesn't know why. Today I became misty eyed so often that I figured he would notice, but I have allergies, so sometimes I can get away with my tears. We saw new places today that would take our breath away. I just wanted all my family and friends in my back seat. I don't know how anyone can look around at the majesty of nature and not know that there is a higher power who makes these awesome presentations to us. Well, Tommy finally saw his bear. If he had not slowed to look at a scene in Shoshone Indian reservation, we may have been picking bear hair from our teeth. He scared the wadding out of me when he yelled, "There it is, there it is!" I saw it about the time he saw us. We braked and he put himself in high gear and headed across the road and into the woods. I know animals are supposed to act on instinct and not have a thought process, but I just know this one was thinking, " Oh my gosh, what is that thing with the two bright eyes doing out here in my yard?" Of course, the buffalo were roaming. Deer and elk were abundant. But, the sweetest thing I saw was as we left our park this morning, a teenage deer came through the drive-through at Burger King. He meandered across the road toward a tavern. Then when we left Wal-mart (again) the deer were standing in the parking lots nibbling. I have been thinking so much today that I will probably be blank tomorrow. But one of my thoughts took me back to my younger years when, although I believed in God, I took him for granted. I remember so well the night that he finally got my attention and will have it forever. We were having a family crisis and I was just simply overwhelmed with fear and with my inability to make things right. Defeat is difficult for me when it comes to my family. I sat in the car numb. Suddenly I literally felt a soft touch on my right shoulder. No one was in that back seat with me or at the time I didn't think so. It was so real that I actually looked to my right shoulder. Then a feeling of peace came over me like I had never experienced in my life. Our crisis did not end immediately, but my way of dealing with it and my family immediately changed. I want to share my prayer with you tonight, please. *Heavenly Father, today I have been full of praise for you and I want to send up these words to let you know how grateful I am for your forgiveness and guiding hand. I hope others recognize your gentle touch, whether it is on their shoulders, their hearts or souls. Thank you for the little fellow you sent us years ago. Thank you for our other son and our grandchildren. Lately, you have taken close family and friends to your side. Just give us the strength to be comfortable knowing that we will see them with you someday. I pray these words in Jesus' precious name and with a humble, grateful heart. Amen.*

July 15th, 2010

We are exhausted. A good tired though. Finished seeing the parts of Yellowstone that we had not visited before and then went back to Old Faithful after 27 years. She is still faithful. I need to correct some info about many of these green crops we see in Montana and Wyoming. Tom Humphrey emailed me. They are crops are sugar beets. He used to live near Cody so he knows many things about this area. He told us, also, that we would love this area and we do. We are only staying five nights, but we could stay for weeks and still be happy seeing and doing new things. I also have a sad note from yesterday. We saw an accident in Yellowstone. A three wheeled motor cycle and an RV hit head on. The only thing showing from the cycle were the back wheels. The driver died. Well, we hit some dirt road today so you know what one of our chores will be tomorrow. I almost needed a nerve pill after viewing Yellowstone Falls. Tommy and I and a small crowd were at the lookout which is surrounded by heavy guard rails. While taking pictures, I noticed a movement to my left about the time that Tommy noticed a child come down over a cliff. He pointed at him and I thought the whole crowd was going to faint. Tommy considered climbing the rail to get him, but was afraid since he has vertigo at heights. People asked him to sit still and where his parents were. He said he didn't know. Folks, below him was the foaming, swift, churning water from the falls. Probably 1500 ft straight down. Everyone convinced him to sit down and not move. Then a tall young man who was speaking French climbed over the rail and retrieved the seven / eight -year-old boy. When his feet hit the pavement he ran up those steps swiftly. As we stopped at another overlook, a lady and I began to talk. I told her of the incident. She described the kid and said as she was coming down a mother was scolding him for disappearing. The lady said she felt the woman did not know about the boy climbing onto the cliff. I will tell you this. If I had seen the mom, I would have told her what he had done. He almost killed himself, but another man could have died trying to rescue him. I will send you a pic and you can see where we were standing. The young man was on the rocks to our left. No bear today, but plenty of bison, huge and small elk and a moose. Museum, blood check, and rodeo tomorrow. Love you all. Night.

July 16th, 2010

Yes, we are still around. Have you missed us? We will have no wifi until 21st at night, probably somewhere in Nebraska. Sorry that you will have so much of us in your mail on one day. Wash day. On our next trip, I will have two prerequisites. One: the park must have cable that broadcasts Fox News, and two: the laundry room must be air- conditioned. I tried to sit in the room and read while my clothes washed and dried. Too hot! I couldn't find shade outside so I decided to pretend I was rich and in a sauna sweating off the pounds. I found a sink with cool water. I just ran water over my arms and dabbed my face. I had two shirts to iron and my sweat dripped on them. Mom, how did you raise 8 kids without electricity? We have one more night in Cody. But, we almost had to wait until Monday to leave. A tire on the trailer was wearing badly. Tommy and the man parked next to us looked over the tire and our neighbor decided that we had a bent axle or worn bearing. They discovered it was a bearing. This man actually had the correct part, grease and tools. While Tommy went to town to have our spare tire put on the wheel, the man fixed everything, and then put everything back together. Tommy called him our Angel. We tried to pay him, but he refused, saying he felt that we were all on this Earth to help take care of each other. Nice. We went to the rodeo last night. Our first one. It was ok, but I worried more about the animals than the cowboys. The horses in the stalls looked so frightened. When they flipped the cows, it had to hurt them. A dust devil blew down the canyon. I even had dust in my ears. The cutest part was when all the kids from the audience, under 12, lined the arena and chased three little calves with ribbons on their tails. The ones who retrieved the ribbons won prizes. Before they turned the calves loose, the clown helped the kids get ready to run. He had them to do jumping jacks, and leg kicks, and then he told them to lie down on their backs and roll from side to side. You should have heard parents in the audience moaning. Then the clown leader told them all to pick up a handful of dirt and put it in their pockets. So cute and funny. Later with love.

July 18th, 2010

On the road today. Headed to Casper. What a beautiful Sunday drive. Drove through Wind Canyon where the Wind River actually runs uphill. The antelope were so numerous. Some had huge black racks. Many were eating the farmers' crops. Farmers pay eight dollars for each antelope that is killed on their farms. We are in a lovely shade spot south of Casper. Don't know the name of the park, but are near Alcova, Wyoming. Our friends who winter near us in Florida have a summer home here on the lake, but live in Casper. What a beautiful area! Pat is fixing trout for supper. I am not a fish eater, but Tommy will be in fish heaven. I'll have the ham. Getting ready for a quick nap before supper. Short note today. Try to give you all a little relief. Buttons and Bows, Buttons and Bows.

July 19th, 2010

Goodness gracious. Just when we thought the beauty was as awesome as it could get, we toured Alcova Canyon from a pontoon boat. Ed and Pat's friends, Jim, Sandy and Braylee, took us on a fabulous ride to see tall multi-colored canyon walls and golden eagles. Then the Cardinals showed us around Casper. I am so amazed at the room people have even in the larger cities. I learned that Wyoming is the 10th largest state in area, but the least populated in our America. I am still loving the sight of the prong horn deer or antelope. Ed and Pat took us to a nice buffet, and I had my first root beer float. The mule deer came for a visit and I was able to entice one to within a few feet of me. She was so pretty. This area has so much history. Tomorrow we will tour some of those places. Remember, if we need to know something important just call.

July 20th, 2010

Off for history lessons today. Saw Independence Rock. This is a large rock where the early pioneers left messages for travelers who were coming behind them. They would sign and date when they were in the area and let people know other landmarks so they could find their way west. Devil's gate is another landmark used by the earlier settlers who were heading to Utah or Oregon. Also, we were at part of the old Oregon Trail. There is even an area nearby where you can view wagon ruts made by the folks in the 1800s. How neat to see. Visited a Morman settlement where they will actually ride you in a cart like they pushed when heading west. Ed and Pat came over to our camp for a Kentucky fried supper. I fried corn, fried cabbage, and fried pork nibblets. I did steam the squash and green beans. I figured I had contributed enough to their artery function without frying the rest of our supper. It was so funny tonight as we socialized , we mentioned a friend whom we grew up with and it seems that Ed and Pat know him also. Don Willoughby lives about 30 miles from us in Florida and he sings and plays music where Pat and Ed live. Headed toward home tomorrow. Should stay in Nebraska the first night. Play it by ear the rest of the way. You all get rid of that hot weather before we get there, please. Sending our love and hugs your way.

July 22nd, 2010

Happy Birthday, Lauren, from Mam and Pap! Just arrived in Jonesburg, MO. Stopped early today so we would not be so exhausted. I don't think you people on my favorites email list are listening to me concerning this weather. It is hot in MO. We have both airs running, I am almost without covering, and Tommy is outside sweating and exploring. Tom Jr. tells us that Friday is going to be terrible too. I will be hovering inside. I do not like hot or cold weather. I know! The folks in Iowa must have had some rain. One part of a road was flooded and the fields were covered in water. Two ducks greeted me at the door just after we arrived. I love ducks, so I took them some of my diet crackers that look like sand paper with a little dry fuzz on them. One duck ate a few bites, gave up and started eating grass. The male (of course) insisted on trying to eat the food. I heard him snort and looked as he began gyrating his head in all directions with his beak hanging open. I thought for a moment that I had killed him, but he recovered and ate a few blades of grass. Then, yes, he came back to peck some more from the ground. I went inside so that if he choked to death, I wouldn't have to watch or be blamed. I must check some things on the net, browse FB, and fix supper. Cooling down in here, finally. Good Night Mrs. Calabash wherever you are.

Back in KY

I'm sorry favorites, but I am so addicted to sharing life with you people that yesterday as I drove two grands home to Bloomfield, I began to laugh and tuck away my thoughts to send your way. We met with Rodney, our last son, who is very limited in his activities so he asked his Dad to go with him to take his son, Anthony, on a fishing adventure to Lake Michigan. Anthony has been a great help to his Dad since Rod's disabilities. I loaded the RV with convenient food and everything I could remember that would help my men enjoy a time of respite. Then all adventures began as they turned north on interstate 65 and I headed south. We began planning our first day. Alex, 8, was so thirsty. Ty, 14, needed to potty. After 24 miles on Bluegrass, we pulled into Wal-mart Bardstown. I stopped to satisfy thirst and for potty, but mainly because I needed to make sure that I still had a steady, substantial heartbeat. Earlier, Ty had inserted a CD that vibrated me from my toes to the tips of my hair. I wanted to be "cool" with my grands, so I smiled and drove. I allowed them to choose, almost everything they wanted to eat, then stopped at the Wal-mart beauty shop to get us all haircuts. As we waited, I recalled the thirst and potty. Alex had bought no drink, Ty forgot to potty. Have you picked up on the "sweet conspiracy"? Then the grands remembered their "needs." After their haircuts, I got my cut while they pottied and went to the drink machines. As we passed the electric carts, Alex asked if I had purchased one yet. He then informed me that I would need one soon. Since we have left the west, a lady has been attacked by a bison in Yellowstone and bears have killed and attacked people in a campground that we passed in Montana.

Phone calls from my boys in Michigan.

Rod: Mom, don't get the kids haircuts at Wal-mart. Pam has other plans.

Ardoth: Oops!

Tommy: Do we have cable here?

Ardoth: No!

Tommy: How do I set up the TV with the antenna?

Ardoth: I don't know

Tommy: The mosquitoes are eating us alive.

Ardoth: SO!

A Barefoot Life

ACKNOWLEDGEMENTS

I have a problem, again. How do I, on one page, love on all the people who have loved on me during my writings. Here is my humble attempt.

God held my hand: thank you Father.

Mom and Dad made me possible: thank you Ernest and Grace Hardin.

Family encouraged and endured: thank you Tommy, Tom Jr., Rod, Pam, Ryan, Lauren, Nick, Anthony, Tyler, Alex, Paul.

Friends insisted, encouraged, and laughed: thank you Joe Britton, Tina/Eddie, Cy/Trisha, Violet/Scoot, Alvin/Wanda, LuAnn/Tony, Ed/Pat, Cree/Gene, Jerry/Jean, Wanda/John, Don/Ilene, Mary/Carlton, Lee/Dan, Don/Jan, Carol/Helga, Elaine/David, Ben/Gay, Deane/Millie, Merileen, Carolyn/Scooter, Jeff, Sherlene/Carol, Joyce, Raleigh/Joann, Jennie, Linda, Paula/Gene, Bonnie, Steve, Robin, Reggie/Sheila, Janet, Gennie, Gloria/Jack, L.B./Naomi, Marilyn/Charles, Dr. Barres, Dorothy/Jack, Ken/Marie, Michelle/Chicken, Cheryl, Fred/Linda, Wanda/ Jerry, Stacy, Sheila, Kay, Talenia, Alda, J.R., Ron/Wanda and last, but so precious, my former students.

I fear that I have forgotten someone. If so, it is not because I don't love you; it is because I am old and limited and still barefoot.

10879921R0

Made in the USA
Lexington, KY
25 August 2011